HOUSING AND THE NATIONAL ECONOMY

The National Institute of Economic and Social Research

OFFICERS OF THE INSTITUTE

2 Dean Trench Street, Smith Square, London, SW1P 3HE

The National Institute of Economic and Social Research is an independent, non–profit–making body, founded in 1938. It has as its aim the promotion of realistic research, particularly in the field of economics. It conducts research by its own research staff and in cooperation with the universities and other academic bodies. The results of the work done under the Institute's auspices are published in several series, and a list of its recent publications will be found at the end of this volume.

Housing and the National Economy

Edited by
JOHN ERMISCH
Senior Research Officer
National Institute of Economic and Social Research

Avebury

Aldershot · Brookfield USA · Hong Kong · Singapore · Sydney

Published by
Avebury
Gower Publishing Company Limited
Gower House
Croft Road
Aldershot
Hants GU11 3HR
England

Gower Publishing Company
Old Post Road
Brookfield
Vermont 05036
USA

ISBN   0 566 07109 6

Printed in Great Britain by
Billing & Sons Ltd, Worcester

Contents

Contributors

David Bell, Department of Political Economy, University of Glasgow

Michael Dicks, Economics Division, Bank of England

John Ermisch, Senior Research Officer, National Institute of Economic and Social Research

Professor Alan W. Evans, Department of Economics, University of Reading

Professor Ian Gordon, Department of Geography, University of Reading

Professor G.A. Hughes, Department of Economics, University of Edinburgh

Christopher Johnson, Chief Economic Adviser, Lloyds Bank plc.

Mark P. Kleinman, Department of Land Economy, University of Cambridge

B. McCormick, Department of Economics, University of Southampton

Professor Duncan Maclennan, Director, Centre for Housing Research, University of Glasgow

Geoffrey P. Meen, Oxford Economic Forecasting

Professor John Muellbauer, Nuffield College, Oxford

Moira Munro, Centre for Housing Research, University of Glasgow

Peter Westaway, Senior Research Officer, National Institute of Economic and Social Research

Christine M.E. Whitehead, London School of Economics

Preface

The contributions to this book are based on papers presented to a conference on Housing and the National Economy organised by the National Institute of Economic and Social Research and held at the Institute on 14 and 15 December 1988. With two exceptions, the chapters are followed by comments made by the discussant of the paper at the conference. A paper presented by Robert Buckley and Stephen Mayo of the World Bank has not been contributed to the volume. It provided examples from a number of different countries of the important macroeconomic impacts of housing policies, and we have included the parallels with the United Kingdom drawn from their paper by the discussant in the comments of Chapter 3. Although there was a lively discussion from the floor throughout, this discussion has not been reported in the book.

The conference was financed by the Housing Finance Research Programme of the Joseph Rowntree Memorial Trust, and the Institute is grateful to them for their support. Duncan Maclennan's contribution at the end of the book places the papers in the context of the Trust's research programme. I am also grateful to the many members of the staff who made the conference run smoothly and to Fran Robinson for copy-editing the papers and preparing them for publication.

John Ermisch
London, March 1989

1 Introduction

Christopher Johnson

There are a number of ways in which housing and the national economy are connected. Housing production is a very important part of the national economy in the sense of its share in investment and national output. It is also a very cyclical component in GDP, which is interest–sensitive. In 1987, somewhere near the peak of the cycle, gross housing investment was 21 per cent of total fixed investment and 3½ per cent of GDP.

Much of the discussion of housing recently has been about the link between house prices and inflation and about the link between housing finance and the monetary side of the economy. The controversy never seems to die down about just how house prices or housing costs should be measured as part of the retail price index (RPI). Instead of measuring house prices directly, we take mortgage interest costs as being the owner–occupied housing component in the RPI. On a couple of occasions the Chancellor of the Exchequer has openly expressed the wish that this was not so, because it makes the RPI a lot more volatile. It means that any government which is using interest rates to damp down general inflation has to start by putting up owner–occupiers' inflation because of mortgage costs.

Going beyond this statistical debate, there has been a theory that house prices and general inflation are connected. Whenever you get a peak in house prices, there seems to be a peak in general inflation shortly afterwards. The last two times that this happened there was also an oil shock, which might have been considered sufficient reason for the rise in the general inflation rate. So it has been very difficult to distinguish the influences. Perhaps the present episode might give us a clearer message, when we get around to analysing it.

There clearly are causal connections running in both directions between wage and price inflation on the one hand, and house prices on the other. There is a reverse connection, in that people's ability to borrow, and finance the purchase of their house, is based on their income levels. They can borrow a multiple of their income level. So rising incomes, other things being equal, are likely to mean higher house prices. Recently, we have often discussed the perhaps more familiar effect whereby higher house prices are thought to have an effect on wage demands, with a strong regional bias towards the south–east. In an economy where wage rates are to some extent nationally set, this may have a wide effect elsewhere in the economy.

Finally, on the subject of house prices and inflation, we can see the effects on consumer spending of increasing borrowing for house purchase, so–called equity withdrawal. We can see also the wealth effect, the effect of rising collateral in both housing and equity investment by the personal sector on spending habits.

The subject of housing and taxation raises many current issues. With almost every type of tax there is some special angle to do with housing.

Mortgage interest relief: Is this a legitimate form of government spending favouring, as it tends to now, people on higher incomes rather than the homeless who might also be thought to have a claim on government funds?

Local taxation: The replacement of rates by the community charge, by removing a tax on housing, will have an upwards effect on house prices. Perhaps it has been rather well timed to offset the expected decline in house prices that may be taking place for other reasons. I don't believe in conspiracy theories. That must be a pure coincidence.

VAT: There is the question of VAT harmonisation in the context of our European Community membership. VAT is leviable on construction, but the British government, like most others in Europe, has chosen to exempt private housing as being a socially desirable objective which doesn't have to be VATed.

Capital tax: We also have a number of issues now being raised in the context of capital and savings taxes, which look like runners in the next budget. The question is whether we haven't got too many exemptions from capital gains tax, in particular the exemptions on owner–occupied housing. Those who advocate an end of this particular tax break have enough political realism to suggest that there should be rollover relief for capital gains when people change houses. So the impact of such a tax will be on those who inherit houses but do not wish to switch into another house if they already have one.

All these issues raise the big question; should we in fact be taxing housing? In a neutral tax system, is it right that there should not actually be a tax specific to housing? We could therefore bring back something like the old schedule A tax based on owner–occupation services. It is not very widely known that the consumption of housing services by owner–occupiers accounts for over 6 per cent of GDP in the analysis of GDP (output). By simply paying ourselves notional rent for living in our own houses, we are making an enormous contribution to GDP. Perhaps that is quite comforting.

Housing policy clearly has wide implications not only for the national economy, but for politics, which is inextricably intertwined with economic issues. There is the question of the availability of land for housebuilding, especially in the south–east. There is the effect on the environment and the side–effects on traffic flows and infrastructure of decisions as to where houses should or should not be built. There are political arguments on both sides. Those who already have pleasant housing in the south–east tend to take a 'nimby' (not in my back yard) attitude, and are somewhat reluctant to be joined by their fellow mortals looking over their garden walls. On the other hand, maybe the national economy requires that more housing accommodation should be found in the south–east, where the demand for labour is.

Another broader issue is housing tenures. There is the obvious interest in and success of the present government's policy in encouraging owner–occupation by maintaining tax concessions and by selling public sector housing at a discount. It is turning us into that famous property–owning democracy, at least with a two–thirds majority, which is usually sufficient to get any government re–elected until kingdom come. There we have the obvious political payoff of the direction in which housing policy is taking us.

There are a few awkward questions left to answer. Even if you don't believe that the public sector should be in the business of renting houses, should we not have a more vigorous private rented sector? This would make labour mobility easier and would fulfil a demand by at least some of those whose favours the government is seeking to attract.

In the next chapter, John Ermisch discusses the main trends in the housing market and in financial markets catering for house purchase. He considers how developments in these markets may have affected the rest of the economy, through their effects on the operation of labour markets and on decisions concerning household consumption and saving. Geoff Meen uses his econometric analysis of the interaction of the markets for housing and housing finance in conjunction with Oxford Economic Forecasting's macroeconomic model to show how policies aimed at the housing market, such as changes in mortgage interest tax relief, affect the housing market and the rest of the economy. He shows that the effects differ depending on whether or not there is rationing in the mortgage market and that interest rate policy becomes a much more potent weapon in the present liberalised mortgage market.

In the following chapter, John Muellbauer discusses impacts of

British housing policies, particularly those directed at the owner–occupied market, on consumption and on interregional migration, unemployment and wage inflation. He outlines a structural reform of the tax treatment of housing which could improve the performance of the economy in a number of respects. In his chapter, Ian Gordon demonstrates how interregional labour migration has become markedly less efficient in equalising unemployment differentials and wage inflation pressures since the late 1970s. He argues, however, that, with the possible exception of the continuing decline of the private rental housing market, housing–related constraints on mobility have had little to do with the decline in geographic mobility; the source of the decline needs to be sought in the labour market itself. Gordon Hughes and Barry McCormick survey the series of studies of mobility and labour markets that they have carried out. These point to important constraints on mobility faced by local authority tenants, contributing to wide regional variation in unemployment rates for manual workers. In contrast to Muellbauer, they do not find any significant effect of regional house prices on migration other than through their effect on regional real wage levels.

It is generally believed that tenants in a rental housing market would be more mobile than either tenants in social housing or owner–occupiers. Christine Whitehead and Mark Kleinman examine whether, in the light of subsidies to owner–occupation and risks, an expanded private rental sector is viable in the United Kingdom. Their analysis indicates that, within current constraints, only large and increasing subsidies to tenants and/or supply subsidies to landlords would produce an expanded private rental sector, and in the absence of these it will continue to decline. In the concluding chapter, Duncan Maclennan places the contributions to this volume in the context of the Joseph Rowntree Memorial Trust's research programme on United Kingdom housing finance and the major housing policy issues.

2 The background: housing trends and issues arising from them

John Ermisch

Introduction

The concern of this chapter, and of the conference it introduced, is not with the social aspects of housing, nor the efficiency of its provision and allocation; it is the interaction of the housing market and housing policies with the operation of the national economy. The first section examines housing market developments, particularly movements in house prices, the factors influencing them, and changes in their differentials between regions. In the second section, financial market developments bringing about the end of mortgage rationing are outlined. The next section discusses how the end of rationing affects the housing market and how changes in house prices and in the mortgage market affect household consumption and saving. Supply–side issues, particularly the interaction of regional housing and labour markets and the consequences for unemployment and wages, are discussed in the fourth section. The chapter concludes with a summary of the main issues.

Key housing market developments

A very important feature of contemporary British housing is the virtual absence of a market for rental housing. This contrasts with many other countries (for example, the United States, the Federal Republic of Germany and the Netherlands) and with Britain in the 1950s, when about a third of houses were rented privately (although many were subject to rent controls), compared to about 8 per cent now. Thus, over the postwar years it became increasingly the case that the only housing *market* is that for owner–occupied housing, and about 65 per cent of households are now owner–occupiers. It is, therefore, not surprising that house prices are the most popular indicator of housing market developments. Furthermore, they play an important role in both demand– and supply–side theories about how the housing market affects the national economy. Thus, their determination and their movements in the past deserve special consideration.

House purchase by owner–occupiers ties the consumption and investment aspects of housing together. In addition to providing a place to live, owner–occupied housing is an asset in a household's portfolio. When an owner–occupier moves, he is both a buyer and a seller in the market, and the decision to move itself is influenced by the price his house will fetch. In the short term, house prices are set through the exchange of the existing housing stock. In this sense, houses are like works of art, soybeans or gilts. But there are important differences. There are large transaction costs in buying and selling houses, there is not a forward market and, in the absence of a rental market, it is almost impossible for households to dramatically reduce their investment in housing. Over the longer term, the housing stock adjusts, and there is a tendency for house prices to converge to the cost of adding another dwelling of a given quality to the stock (for example, see the model in Appendix 2.1.).

National average house prices in real and nominal terms are shown in chart 2.1. These series, compiled by Alan Holmans (1988), give the longest–term view presently available. There are a number of interesting features of postwar house price developments.

Most striking is the pattern of sharp fluctuations in *real* house prices during the 1970s and 1980s. These mainly reflect fluctuations in the demand for owner–occupied housing, which are magnified by changes in expectations about the returns from investment in it. To illustrate this, consider a household that maximises lifetime utility (with housing and other consumption being the goods entering the intertemporal utility function) and does not face a binding borrowing constraint. Its marginal user cost of owner–occupied housing is

$$\text{UCH} = [i(1-t) + \tau + \delta - dP_H^e/P_H]P_H/P) \tag{1}$$

where i is the mortgage interest rate, t is the household's marginal income tax rate, τ is the effective rate of property tax (rates), δ is depreciation and maintenance as a proportion of house value, P_H/P is the real asset price of housing, and dP_H^e/P_H is the expected nominal capital gain on owner–occupied housing. If the household's mortgage exceeds the tax relief ceiling of £30,000, then, in effect, $t=0$ in (1). If the household has no mortgage, then i refers to the return on financial assets.

Increases in the expected capital gain lower UCH and raise the demand for owner–occupied housing. Because housing supply is fixed in the short term, changes in demand are initially reflected only in changes

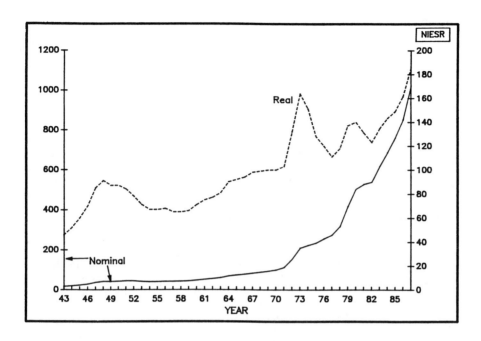

Chart 2.1 Nominal and real house prices (1970=100)
Source: Holmans (1988), tables A.1 and A.2
Note:Adjusted from 1983 to include houses purchased with a bank loan.

in house (and land) prices. It is plausible that such expectations are more volatile than changes in housing demand arising from changes in income and in the number of households, thereby leading to sharp fluctuations in real house prices. How these expectations are formed, including their time horizon, is a difficult question, and one that needs to be addressed in modelling the dynamics of house prices (see, for example, Hendry, 1984 and Meen, 1987).

A second feature is the rarity of falls in *nominal* house prices during the past 45 years. Falls only occurred during 1948–9 and between 1951 and 1954. Perhaps the absence of nominal house price decline since the mid–1950s reflects a strong secular increase in housing demand in response to rising incomes and growth in the number of households, or it may have been fortuitous that general inflation has always been sufficiently rapid during periods of decline in demand for owner–occupied housing that real house prices could adjust without nominal declines. But the peculiar features of the market for secondhand houses mentioned earlier could also produce an asymmetry in the response of house prices to changes in the prospective returns (including imputed income and capital gains) from owner–occupied housing.

7

When these expected returns are favourable relative to other assets, households want to increase their investment in housing. They do so by trading up to a larger degree when they move, and they also may bring moves forward. Tenants and newly formed households also become owners to obtain these high returns. This fuels increases in nominal house prices. Near the peak of the house price boom, when expected housing capital gains drop dramatically, financial motives would encourage households to adjust their portfolios in favour of other assets. One way it could do this is by trading down in house value. But large transaction costs discourage this, and in order to adjust in a major way, households must be able to move into housing that they do not own, which is difficult in Britain. Furthermore, households with a mortgage that is a large percentage of house value are probably reluctant to sell their house at a lower nominal price, and so they postpone moving house. Large and rapid nominal falls in house prices are discouraged by this behaviour, but clearly real falls can occur when stagnant nominal house prices are accompanied by general inflation.

This does not mean that large declines in nominal house prices are impossible, but they appear unlikely as long as underlying housing demand arising from income growth and household formation remains strong and general inflation is moderate to high. Certainly the historical evidence is consistent with this view.

A third feature of house price history is the emergence of an upward trend in *real* house prices after 1960. While the real house price series shown in chart 2.1 is not adjusted for changes in the quality of the housing stock, the upward trend does not merely reflect better quality houses. Calculations by Holmans (1988) show that even after adjusting for quality changes a strong upward trend remains. Given that it is likely that housing supply is not perfectly elastic with respect to price, increases in the number of households and in their disposable income could readily account for such a trend.

The trend rate of increase in quality–adjusted house prices is, however, less than the rate of increase in disposable income. This contrasts with a common view that there is some natural ratio of house prices to income (or earnings), to which house prices adjust. The simple model of a housing market developed in Appendix 2.1 shows that whether house prices or income increase more rapidly over the longer term depends on the income and price elasticities of housing demand, the elasticity of residential land supply and the elasticity of substitution between land and other inputs (labour and materials) in the production of housing. It would take a favourable constellation of the elasticities to produce a long–run ratio of house prices to income that is constant. A slower rise in house prices than in disposable income is more likely, the larger are these two supply–side elasticities and the price elasticity of housing demand relative to the income elasticity of housing demand.

Another likely influence on house prices is the supply of public sector housing. This housing is generally let at rents below full cost, with rationing by queues. At least on a theoretical level, we would expect a larger public sector housing stock to reduce queues, the demand for owner–occupied housing and house prices, and Buckley and Ermisch (1982) show evidence of such an effect. In addition to these overspill effects on the owner–occupied market, the proportion of households in public sector housing is of interest in its own right, particularly because local authority tenants consistently have been found to be less geographically mobile than other households (see, for example, Hughes and McCormick, Chapter 6).

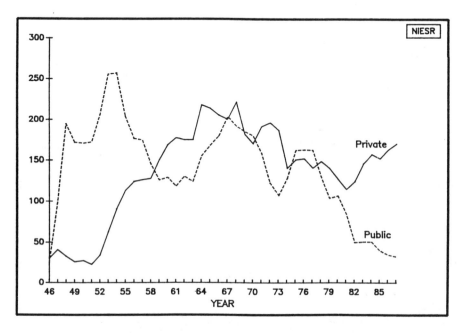

Chart 2.2 Housing completions (thousands)
Source:Economic Trends.

From their peak in 1979, the number of local authority dwellings in Great Britain declined by 680,000 to 26.7 per cent of all dwellings at the end of 1986.   The sale of 1.06 million dwellings during this period is primarily responsible for the decline, although the steep decline in public sector housebuilding during this period, shown in chart 2.2, was a contributory factor.   The sales to sitting tenants have had little direct impact on the market for owner–occupied housing, but the fact that new housebuilding for the public sector has lagged behind household formation (see chart 2.3) has probably increased demand for owner–occupied housing and house prices.

In addition, there was a   dramatic increase in public sector rents at the beginning of the 1980s.   In real terms, rents increased by 44 per cent during 1980–82, since when they have been relatively constant.   This probably encouraged tenants to become owner–occupiers, and this may increase house prices as well as shortening queues for public housing (for example, Weibull's (1983) model suggests such an impact).

The private rental sector continued its decline, with a reduction of about 500,000 dwellings since 1981. A substantial proportion of these probably were subject to rent regulation or control. The reduction tends to increase demand for owner–occupied housing and house prices and to lengthen local authority queues. Because only about 175,000 dwellings in total were demolished during these years, it appears that a vast majority of the reduction in private rental dwellings can be accounted for by sales into owner occupation. Such sales have an offsetting supply effect in the owner–occupied market.

The smaller stock of private rental housing may also reduce the opportunities for mobility in the population. In the past, this sector has played an important role for recent movers to an area, providing transitional housing before purchase or obtaining a local authority dwelling.

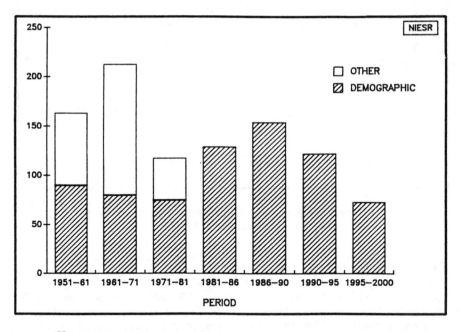

Chart 2.3 Growth in households per annum (thousands)
Source: Actual household growth during 1951–81 is derived from the Censuses.
Note: 'Demographic' refers to changes in the number of households in Great Britain arising from changes in the age/sex distribution of the population. Here, the population is weighted by using 1971 household headship rates for 1951–81 and 1981 headship rates for 1981–2000.

Another form of social housing, rationed at rents below full cost, is provided by housing associations. While the stock of these dwellings has expanded, the increase has provided little offset to the fall in other rental housing, increasing by only 128,000 between April 1981 and December 1986 to 2.5 per cent of the housing stock. During that same period, changes in the age distribution alone would have added about 600,000 households (see chart 2.3).

The widening gap between house prices in the north and south of Great Britain has received considerable attention in recent years. At first glance, this attention is somewhat surprising because since 1968, after which regional house price data has been readily available, regional house price differentials have always widened during periods when house prices have risen more rapidly than the general rate of price inflation. In particular, when house prices have increased rapidly, house prices in the south–east have risen relative to those of the northern regions. But when house price inflation slowed down, the other regions caught up again, so that the interregional house price relativities tended to be restored.

For instance, until 1986, house prices in northern regions relative to the south–east (excluding London) were above those experienced during 1972, another boom period. Since then however, northern house prices

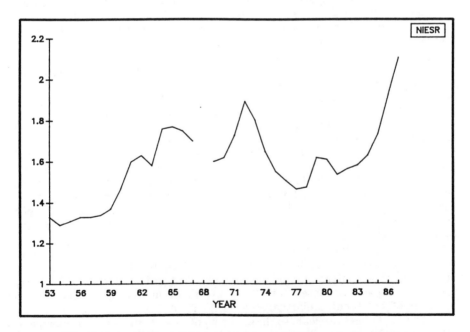

Chart 2.4 Ratio of house prices, south–east to north
Sources: 1953–67, Holmans (1988), table B.7; 1969–87, *Housing and Construction Statistics* and Holmans (1988), table B.1.

have fallen to unprecedented lows relative to the south–east. Will this be reversed now that national house price inflation has slowed down?

Recent analysis by Alan Holmans (1988) shows that the longer–term stability of regional differences in house prices suggested by the experience during 1968–86 was not evident in earlier years. Chart 2.4 illustrates the widening of differentials in house prices between the south–east and the north during 1958–65. It is possible that the years 1965–82 were an anomaly and that 1982–8 may be a period like 1958–65, producing an upward shift in interregional house price differences. Given the likelihood that residential land supply is less elastic in the south of England, especially around London, a secular upward trend in north–south differences is plausible. But the demand side cannot be neglected. What role did industrial depression in the north (and during 1982–8 in the midlands), relative to prosperity in the south, play in the widening of house price differentials during 1958–65 and 1982–8?

Financial market developments associated with housing

The greater intensity of competition for retail funds and in mortgage and consumer credit markets during the 1980s is a crucially important development for the housing market and for its interaction with the economy. A catalyst in this development was the large scale re–entry of banks into the mortgage market after the abolition in mid–1980 of corset controls on their balance sheet growth. In 1979, banks held about 5 per cent of outstanding mortgage debt. By the end of 1982, they had increased their share to 14 per cent, and at the end of 1987 they held 19.5 per cent of mortgage debt.

The competition from banks forced changes in the behaviour of building societies, the most important of which being the adoption of the aim of meeting mortgage demand rather than protecting existing borrowers from interest rate changes. This made societies more sensitive to changes in market interest rates and intensified competition for retail funds between societies, including the break–up of their interest rate cartel. As banks and building societies moved up the supply curve for retail savings, share and deposit rates, mortgage rates and lending increased. Also, building societies significantly decreased their reliance on the retail market for funds, with over 10 per cent of their funds coming from the wholesale market in each year since 1983 (32 per cent in 1986), and by the end of 1987 such borrowing made up 9 per cent of their liabilities.

Other financial institutions, such as mortgage corporations, who rely on wholesale funds, have been attracted to the market by the high profitability of mortgage lending in this competitive market. In 1987, these institutions accounted for 13.5 per cent of net advances and held 4 per cent of outstanding mortgages at the end of 1987.

These changes appear to have brought about the end of mortgage rationing. Estimates of mortgage rationing based on aggregate data constructed by Meen (1985) suggest rationing ended during the early 1980s. Information on the distribution of first-time buyers' mortgage

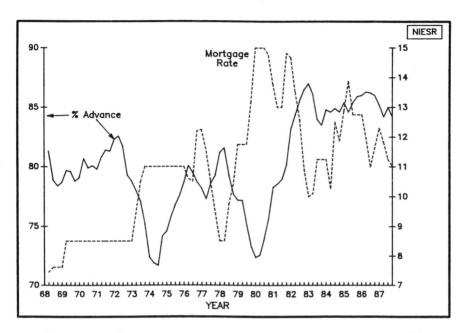

**Chart 2.5 First–time buyers' average percentage advance(%)
and mortgage rate (%)**
Sources: BSA Bulletin and *Housing and Construction Statistics.*

advances as a per cent of house value (percentage advance) suggests a
significant change in lending behaviour in 1982. During 1978–81, only
between 5 and 20 per cent of first–time buyers borrowed 94 per cent or
more of house value. In 1982, nearly 50 per cent borrowed this much, and
during 1983–7 around 50 per cent borrowed 95–100 per cent. Indeed, about
a quarter had 100 per cent mortgages in these years.

This shift in behaviour is also clear in chart 2.5, in which the
ratio of first–time buyers' average advance to their average house price
is plotted over a longer period. From 1982 on it remains at a much
higher level than previously. Furthermore, chart 2.5 also shows that a
negative association between mortgage rates and first–time buyers'
advance to house price ratio existed during 1968–83. This is consistent
with rationing in this period, because if mortgage rates do not fully
follow market rates upward (to protect existing borrowers), then
rationing would be stronger when interest rates are higher. But this
relationship breaks down after 1983, again suggesting that rationing
ended during the early 1980s.

Demand–side issues
The way in which housing market developments affect aggregate demand in

Housing and the National Economy

the economy depends crucially on whether there is mortgage rationing or not. Some insight into why this is so can be obtained from the simple model of household lifetime utility maximisation mentioned earlier. If the household faces a binding borrowing constraint, then its user cost of housing becomes

$$UCH = [i(1-t) + \tau + \delta - dP_H^e/P_H + \mu/\lambda_1](P_H/P) \qquad (2)$$

where μ is the shadow price associated with the borrowing constraint and λ_1 is the marginal utility of income in the present period. Furthermore, the price of present consumption relative to future consumption is

$$PPC = 1 + i(1-t) - \pi + \mu/\lambda_2 \qquad (3)$$

where π is the expected rate of price inflation and λ_2 is the marginal utility of income in the next period. Utility maximisation entails that the marginal rate of substitution between housing and other consumption equals UCH and the marginal rate of substitution between present and future consumption equals PPC.

When rationing is in force and the borrowing constraint is binding ($\mu>0$), general increases in demand, generated for instance by increases in wealth, or an increase in housing demand, produced for instance by higher expected capital gains on housing assets (higher dP_H^e/P_H) also increase μ, thereby tending to dampen the increase in demand through an increase in UCH and PPC. By eliminating the borrowing constraint (making $\mu=0$), the removal of rationing has a one-off effect that raises the demand for both housing and present consumption. But in addition, housing demand and consumption are more responsive to factors like wealth increases and changes in expected capital gains than when rationing was in force. Chapter 3 estimates some of these effects.

Higher house prices increase the wealth of owner–occupiers. Thus aggregate consumption would be expected to increase with house prices. When rationing was in force, the response would have been dampened by the borrowing constraint, but after the end of rationing, consumption should be more responsive to changes in house prices.

An indication that consumption may have become more responsive to house price changes after mortgage rationing ended is the sharp increase in the amount of equity withdrawal by moving owner–occupiers with mortgages after 1981, shown in table 2.1. This undoubtedly also reflects upward adjustments to households' desired level of mortgage borrowing, which they formerly were constrained from achieving because of rationing. This adjustment would be likely to be spread over a considerable period because it is cheaper (particularly if the mortgage is below £30,000) to do this when moving house, and owner–occupiers only move every five to seven years on average.

It is not, however, necessary to mortgage the increment in house value in order for house prices to affect consumption. The fact that households know that they can easily borrow on the basis of their housing wealth if necessary (note the spread of lines of credit based on housing equity) may make them more willing to draw down their liquid assets or

14

use consumer credit to finance consumption when house prices increase.

These arguments imply that the effect of house prices on consumption, indeed the effect of wealth and other variables in the consumption function, is likely to have changed in the 1980s because of the end of mortgage rationing and the new environment for consumer credit. Another implication of these arguments is that the savings rate, as conventionally measured, may fall as house prices increase.

But the net change in the savings rate need not be downwards, because higher house prices tend to transfer wealth from younger (recent purchasers) to older (aged 45–60) households, who have higher propensities to save. They also increase the transfers of wealth arising from deaths of owner–occupiers (see, for example, the first column of table 2.1). These bequests are, on average, to persons in their fifties, who are likely to save a large proportion of the transfer. If these bequests are treated like a windfall, the permanent income hypothesis would suggest that they go entirely into saving. On the other hand, at least a proportion of the bequest is probably already reflected in the heirs' permanent income and consumption. Whatever the net effect, the upward trend in home ownership across generations and the ageing of the population will continue to increase transfers of wealth from sales of the houses of deceased owner–occcupiers.

House price changes are not, of course, an exogenous influence on consumption. Part of the 1982–8 house price boom is itself a reflection of the one–off effect of the end of rationing on housing demand, as suggested by equation (2). For the reasons discussed above in connection

Table 2.1 Equity withdrawal from owner–occupiers' house purchase transactions

Year	Last–time sellers		Moving owner–occupiers		Total
	Elderly households dissolved	Other	Without mortgages	With mortgages	(Narrow defin–ition[a]
1977	1,425	830	325	725	3,305
1978	1,730	1,035	380	910	4,055
1979	2,145	1,250	455	960	4,810
1980	2,390	1,325	455	925	5,095
1981	2,850	1,540	470	1,490	6,350
1982	3,265	1,965	535	3,640	9,405
1983	3,695	2,135	530	2,990	9,350
1984	4,555	2,805	445	2,575	10,380

Source: Holmans (1986), table 4.
[a]Corresponds to Holmans' definition in table 8, and it refers to equity withdrawal arising from the change of ownership of existing owner–occupied houses.

with adjusting mortgage borrowing, the upward adjustment of housing demand may be spread over a long period. But stronger housing demand responses probably also play a role in the boom.

The analysis at the outset of this section also implies that the responses of demand for owner–occupied housing and house prices to changes in income, price expectations, and so on have been stronger after rationing ended in the early 1980s. As noted earlier (in relation to equation (1)), the dynamics of house prices are likely to be a strong reflection of expected future changes in house prices. Because of the upward adjustment in housing demand after the end of rationing, and also because of rapid growth in real earnings among non–manual employees (averaging 3.1 per cent per annum during 1979–87) and the acceleration of household formation arising from age distribution changes (see chart 2.3), there was a strong underlying increase in housing demand during the 1980s. Once house prices started increasing in response, expectations of future rises were enhanced, thereby reducing the user cost of housing (dP_H^e/P_H in equation (1) or (2) increased) and reinforcing the increase in housing demand and house prices. The absence of rationing strengthened the response to these expectations. Higher housing demand increased the demand for mortgages, raising mortgage borrowing in step with house prices. Thus, it is likely that rising mortgage credit merely played the role of facilitator, allowing the housing demand to respond to the underlying increase and to the expectations engendered by it.

In this view, rising mortgage credit plays no causal role in the house price boom. Its causes lie in the removal of mortgage rationing and the increase in incomes and household formation, the effects of which on house prices were magnified through the formation of expectations. To attribute the cause to rising mortgage credit could be likened to attributing the cause of a trip to work as the underground train, when it really lies in the need to eat.

This contrasts with the role of mortgage credit during rationing. The amount of mortgage borrowing was then determined by what building societies were willing to lend at the mortgage rate they had set, rather than by the interaction of the demand for credit with its supply. Thus, under rationing, mortgage lending did have a causal role to play in house price movements.

It is clear from equation (2) that the forthcoming abolition of rates lowers the user cost of housing, thereby providing a further upward impetus to house prices. The extent to which this has already been reflected in housing demand and house prices is, however, unclear. Looking further ahead, chart 2.3 shows that age distribution changes produce strong deceleration in household formation during the 1990s. This reflects the replacement of the baby boom generation in the household forming ages by the baby bust generation (born during the 1970s).

The absence of a rental housing market means that households bear more risk than they would otherwise, which may affect their other economic behaviour. Owner–occupiers must put a large proportion of their savings in one asset, the real price of which is subject to fluctuation. Indeed, if nominal house prices were to fall, the substantial proportion of borrowers with high loan–to–value ratios could owe more than their house is worth, and they would be encouraged to default if there is rental housing in which to move. While they are presently diversifying, building societies continue to have about 80 per cent of their assets in mortgages, making them very vulnerable to such defaults, but the absence of a rental market makes it less likely that they would occur.[1]

Supply-side issues

One aspect of the influence of housing on the supply side of the economy is the effect of housing finance policies on the relative after–tax rates of return on different assets, which affect investment decisions. For instance, the implicit subsidies to owner–occupied housing through the tax system encourage over–investment in owner–occupied housing, particularly at the upper end of the market. To the extent that there is a housing supply response, this would tend, all else being equal, to reduce investment in other parts of the economy yielding a higher pre–tax rate of return. For example, Hendershott and Hu (1981) have argued that the interaction of the United States tax treatment of owner–occupied housing (similar to that in the United Kingdom) with inflation during the 1970s distorted capital allocation in favour of owner–occupied housing and reduced productivity growth.

It is difficult to assess the quantitative importance of this in the United Kingdom economy because other investments, particularly through pension funds, also receive favourable treatment, which may offset the tax advantages of investing in owner–occupied housing. Furthermore, the housing supply response to higher prices appears to be much more limited in the United Kingdom than in the United States, thereby reducing any resource misallocation resulting from these tax advantages.

Probably more important, particularly in relation to the mobility issues raised below, owner–occupied housing's tax advantage discourages investment in rental housing. Even in the absence of rent controls, an owner–occupier would be willing to pay a higher price for a given dwelling than a landlord because of the former's tax advantages. This is one of the reasons that houses with vacant possession are sold into owner occupation. Clearly rent regulations and controls or the risk of their future imposition also reduce the value of dwellings to landlords and discourage their rental (see Chapter 8 for a fuller discussion).

The role of housing allocation systems in labour mobility has been the subject of considerable discussion and analysis. Hughes and McCormick (1981,1985,1987) have produced evidence suggesting that the rent–setting and allocation mechanisms in local authority housing impede the geographic mobility of manual workers. In sharp contrast to the United States, they find job–related migration is greater for non–manual workers than manual in Britain. Minford *et al* (1988) contend that discouragement of labour migration caused by controls in the rental market and the council house system produces larger regional differences in manual workers' wages and unemployment rates than is the case for non–manual workers, and a higher national rate of unemployment.

Bover, Muellbauer and Murphy (1988) argue that regional differences in house prices have similar effects: As house prices rise in prosperous labour markets (the south) relative to less prosperous ones (the north), this discourages mobility to the prosperous regions, which prompts faster wage inflation and a higher level of unemployment than would otherwise be the case. The rise in house prices in the south is magnified by owner–occupiers' tax advantages and by the effect of house price expectations mentioned earlier. At least initially, when house prices are increasing rapidly, outward migration from the south may also be discouraged, further stimulating the rise. Similarly, after house prices peak in the south, southerners are more willing to migrate, but the expectation of lower capital gains in the south may discourage migration from the north, thereby adding to southern wage pressure. These dynamics suggest that southern house price overshooting and wage pressure will be magnified (see Chapter 4).

An important source of these dynamics is the difficulty in separating the investment aspect of housing expenditure from that of consumption. At present, an owner–occupier moving to a region with a lower expected rate of house price increase would generally have to shift a major part of his wealth to an asset earning an inferior rate of return. He would only move if his better prospects in the region, including a lower *level* of house prices, were expected to outweigh his lower return on investments. In contrast, if there were a freer market in rental housing, he could separate his investment decisions from his labour market ones (for instance, keeping and letting his house in the higher return area and renting in the new location). The freer movement of capital and people in this situation would also tend to reduce regional differences in house prices. Thus, the lack of a market in rental housing may be more important than the fiscal reliefs associated with owner–occupation in creating the dynamic responses to regional differentials in economic prosperity suggested by Bover *et al* (1988).[2]

In the longer run, the house price differential could be expected to encourage people and firms to move to the north, thereby reducing unemployment in the north, wage pressure in the south, and the house price differential. But Bover *et al* (1988) argue that the dynamics involved in reaching this position, outlined above, can be very costly. In other words, even if a new regional equilibrium is attained in the long run, the costs of getting there under present housing policies are large.

Whether housing and labour markets interact in this way depends on migration being responsive to house price differentials. The reestablishment of an equilibrium after a shock depends, however, on regional migration not being too responsive to house prices. To illustrate, Appendix 2.2 presents a simple model of interaction between a region's housing and labour markets. The primary source of the interdependence between housing and labour markets is the fact that migration, thereby regional labour supply, depends in part on wages and house prices, while housing demand depends on the size of the regional population as well as wages (income) and house prices.

The simple model shows that, even in the absence of rent controls, housing subsidies and administrative allocation of housing, the two markets could interact in a way which causes instability in regional economies, manifesting itself in wage and house price inflation in some regions (for example, southern England) and a higher rate of unemployment in the national economy. The chances of that happening depends on a number of parameters. Stability is more likely the more responsive is migration to wages and the less responsive it is to house prices. The likelihood of stability also is higher the larger are the elasticity of the demand for labour, the price elasticity of the demand for housing and the price elasticity of housing supply, and the smaller is the income elasticity of housing demand.

It is, however, shown in Appendix 2.2 that even if regional migration is as responsive to house prices as to *nominal* wages, stability is assured for plausible values of the price and income elasticities of the demand for housing and the price elasticity of housing supply. If migration responds to *real* wages, we would expect the elasticity of migration to house prices to be only a fraction of its elasticity to nominal wages, the fraction being roughly equal to the share of housing in household budgets (perhaps about 0.25).

Nevertheless, the nature of dynamic housing–labour market interactions depends on the responsiveness of migration to house price differentials. Chart 2.6 plots movements of migration between the south–east and the rest of the United Kingdom exclusive of East Anglia and the south–west (because a substantial part of moves to these two regions are moves within the same labour market) and the ratio of average house price in the south–east to that in the rest of the United Kingdom. Although factors other than the house price differential undoubtedly affect migration, a bivariate relationship between the relative house price in the south–east and north–south migration should be visible if migration is strongly responsive to house price differentials, particularly because the variance in relative house prices is probably much greater than that of other potential explanatory variables, like relative earnings.

Migration *from* the south–east appears to be larger when house prices are higher in the south–east relative to elsewhere, but, surprisingly, migration *into* the south–east also appears to be *larger* when house prices are relatively higher in the south–east. Regression analyses bear these relationships out, and they also suggest that migration from the south–east is smaller and in-migration is larger when the rate of relative house price inflation is faster.[3] These latter dynamic relations are consistent with the role of expected housing capital gains in housing demand and migration suggested earlier.

The odd positive relationship between in-migration and relative

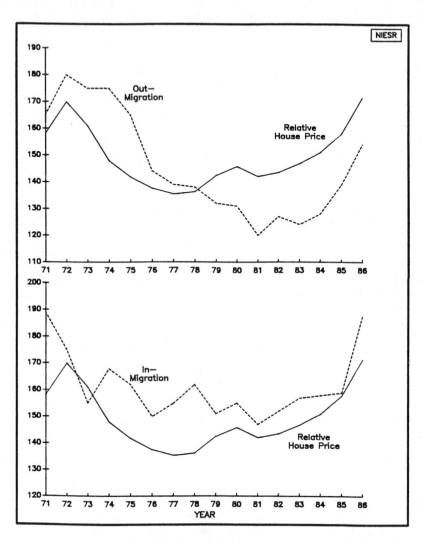

**Chart 2.6 Relative house price in the south–east
and migration from and to the south–east**

Sources: *Housing and Construction Statistics* for house prices and
migration data from Holmans (1988), table 20.

Note: Relative house price in the south–east is the average house price
in the south–east, including London, relative to the weighted average
house price in the rest of the country (equality=100). Migration flows in
thousands.

house prices could reflect the impact of in–migration on south–east house prices, but tests for the exogeneity of the relative house price suggest that it can be treated as exogenous in the in–migration equation.[4] It could also reflect a feedback effect from out–migration, a higher level of which could encourage more in–migration. This can only be sorted out by more rigorous modelling of migration flows. Preliminary reports of such analysis by Muellbauer and Murphy (1988a) indicate that relative house prices do indeed have a negative effect on migration to the south–east in an econometric model including other variables influencing migration, as well as a positive effect on out–migration.

Thus, there appears to be evidence that migration from the south–east is encouraged by higher relative house prices there, and that migration to the south–east is discouraged by higher relative house prices, although the latter is not clear from a simple bivariate relationship. But even the simple analysis here does indicate that the long–term effect of higher relative house prices in the south–east is to reduce *net* migration to the south–east. Similar results were obtained when migration flows between East Anglia and the south–west and the south–east were included.

It was suggested above that some of the costly dynamics arise because of the absence of a rental market. Furthermore, while owner–occupiers may be more mobile than local authority tenants, there are large transaction costs associated with owner–occupiers' moves. House moves in a rental *market* would generally involve lower transaction costs. Thus, a question related to both the mobility and investment distortion issues concerns the possibility of expanding rental housing outside the local authority sector. Such an expansion would improve labour mobility if the costs of moving in this rental sector were lower, and this appears more likely if a better private rental market were to develop. What sort of rates of return would be required to attract private investment in rental housing, either run by housing associations or by private companies or individuals? What effect would different managements of rental housing have on labour mobility? Chapter 7 addresses some of these issues.

The final issue considered concerns the impact of planning policies on the interaction between housing and labour markets and on aggregate demand in the economy. These policies tend to reduce residential land supply and its responsiveness to price, particularly in the more prosperous south–east. A lower price elasticity of residential land supply lowers the price elasticity of housing supply (see Appendix 2.1), which in turn makes it more likely that housing and labour markets interact in an unstable way (see Appendix 2.2) and exacerbates the costly dynamics of labour market adjustment suggested by Bover *et al.* By magnifying the rise in house prices associated with any given rise in housing demand, a lower price elasticity of housing supply enlarges the effects of housing demand changes on consumption and saving discussed earlier.

Also, to the extent that house price increases are passed on in higher wages and salaries, international competitiveness is adversely affected, and multinational firms may be discouraged from locating in the United Kingdom because of these higher costs. Consumers suffer welfare losses in being forced to consume less space than they would in the absence of these constraints on residential land supply. Obviously, these costs, and others not operating through the housing market (see Evans, 1988), must be set against the perceived benefits from the planning policies.

Conclusion

A number of important issues have emerged from this review. To what extent are consumption and saving decisions affected by changes in house prices in the new financial market catering for house purchase? Has the end of mortgage rationing produced a structural shift in consumption and saving behaviour? On the supply side of the economy, what effects do regional housing market developments and housing tenure mix have on labour market adjustment, wages and unemployment?

The absence of a rental market has come up many times in the discussion. It was argued that it affects the nature of house price movements (with effects on consumption and saving), the risks faced by households, and labour mobility. That is why the viability of a rental housing market, or some substitute providing rental housing on a flexible basis, is such an important issue.

Appendix 2.1: A simple model of a housing market

The purpose of the model is to characterise a long–run housing market equilibrium in which all demand and supply adjustments have been completed and to examine how such an equilibrium changes with different steady–state values of exogenous variables. The main economic agents in the model are consumers, housebuilders and owners of land.

Let P_H be the price of a dwelling unit of given quality Q_0, with housing quality being produced by the production function $Q=F(L,\alpha N)$, where L is the amount of land, N is the amount of other inputs (for example, labour) and α is a factor augmenting the productivity of N. It is assumed that the housebuilder minimises the cost of producing such a dwelling; that is, he minimises $wN+P_L L$ subject to $Q_0=F(L,\alpha N)$, where P_L and w are the prices of land and non–land inputs respectively. This entails that

$$w/\alpha F_N = P_L/F_L \qquad (A1)$$

where F_L and αF_N are the marginal products of land and non–land inputs respectively. From these conditions of cost minimisation, we can derive a demand function for residential land in terms of (small) percentage changes:

$$dlogL_d = -\sigma S_N dlogP_L + \sigma S_N dlog(w/\alpha) + dlogH \qquad (A2)$$

where σ is the elasticity of substitution between land and other inputs; S_N is the share of the cost of inputs other than land in total costs; and H is the number of dwelling units of quality Q_0 built. The demand function of other inputs to housing production takes a similar form.

The supply of land for residential use is assumed to be purely a function of its price:

$$dlogL_s = \gamma dlogP_L \qquad (A3)$$

where γ is the elasticity of land supply.

The aggregate demand for housing of quality Q_0 is assumed to be given by the following function:

$$dlogH_d = \beta dlogX - \phi dlog(UCH) \qquad (A4)$$

where UCH is the user cost of housing given in equation (1) of the text and can be expressed as $UCH=RP_H$, where R is the quantity in brackets on the right–hand side of (1); ϕ is the price elasticity of housing demand; X represents non–price influences on housing demand, like average income and the number of households, and β is the elasticity with respect to X (for example, income elasticity if X is income).

In long–run equilibrium, building firms will enter the market and existing firms will expand output until profits are eliminated; that is,

$$P_HH = wN + P_LL \qquad (A5)$$

In this equilibrium, annual housing production is proportional to the housing stock, the factor of proportionality being the annual replacement rate. Using the input demand functions, the long–run equilibrium condition (A5) entails that

$$dlogP_H = S_Ndlog(w/\alpha) + S_LdlogP_L \qquad (A6)$$

where $S_L=1-S_N$ is the share of land costs in the total costs of a dwelling unit. Furthermore, the residential land market will be in equilibrium $(L_s=L_d)$.

Before proceeding to the comparative statics, it is helpful to develop an expression for the price elasticity of housing supply. In general, a price elasticity of supply measures the responsiveness to output price changes when input prices are held constant. But in long–run equilibrium, the no profits condition (A5) must hold, and it is necessary to consider the impact of demand on the prices of inputs not perfectly elastic in supply, in this case residential land. Assuming that other inputs are perfectly elastic in supply, the long–run housing supply elasticity can be derived by setting $dlog(w/\alpha)=0$ in (A2) and (A6) and using (A3) and the land market equilibrium condition. It then follows from the definition of supply elasticity $(=dlogH/dlogP_H)$ that the elasticity of housing supply (ε) is given by

Housing and the National Economy

$$\varepsilon = (\sigma S_N + \gamma)/S_L \tag{A7}$$

These relationships entail the following comparative static equations for P_H, P_L and H:

$$dlogP_H = [-\phi dlogR + \beta dlogX]/(\varepsilon + \phi)$$

$$+ [S_N(\varepsilon + \sigma)/(\varepsilon + \phi)]dlog(w/\alpha) \tag{A8}$$

$$dlogP_L \doteq [-\phi dlogR + \beta dlogX]/(\varepsilon + \phi)S_L$$

$$+ [S_N(\sigma - \phi)/(\varepsilon + \phi)S_L]dlog(w/\alpha) \tag{A9}$$

$$dlogH = [-\varepsilon\phi/(\varepsilon + \phi)]dlogR$$

$$+ [\beta\varepsilon/(\varepsilon + \phi)]dlogX - \phi[S_N(\varepsilon + \sigma)/(\varepsilon + \phi)]log(w/\alpha) \tag{A10}$$

We want to examine the implications of long–run growth in real income at a rate of g*100 per cent per annum for the rate of change in real house prices, P_H. One plausible assumption about the rate of change in the price of other inputs in housing production is that it grows at the same rate as their productivity grows, so that dlogw=dlogα. Thus setting dlog(w/α)=0=dlogR in (A8) and letting X be income,

$$dlogP_H = \beta g/(\varepsilon + \phi) \tag{A11}$$

and the change in the ratio of house prices to income is

$$dlog(P_H/X) = dlogP_{II} - g = [\beta - \varepsilon - \phi]g/(\varepsilon + \phi) \tag{A12}$$

It is clear from (A8) that if dlogw > dlogα, then a positive term is added to the right hand side of (A12). Thus, under the very plausible condition that the productivity of other inputs in housing production (for example, labour) does not grow faster than their price, *a necessary condition for the house price to income ratio to show a secular decline* is that $\beta < \varepsilon + \phi$, or equivalently, $\beta < [(\sigma S_N + \gamma)/S_L + \phi]$.

Appendix 2.2: A simple model of regional housing and labour market interactions

In order to illustrate the interrelationship between a region's housing and labour markets, we consider a simple equilibrium model for one region. Multi–regional equilibrium is not considered. It is probably one of the simplest models that entails interesting labour market interactions. All variables are expressed in logarithms for convenience.

Firms are assumed to be footloose in the sense that transport costs are not an important locational consideration and they sell their products on a national or world market. The price of their basket of products is taken to be the numeraire. Their demand for labour is given by

$$L^d = d - cw \qquad (A2.1)$$

where w is the product wage paid by firms (c and all other slope parameters are defined to be positive).

The supply of labour is given by

$$L^s = a + b_1(w - s_0p) - b_2p_h \qquad (A2.2)$$

where s_0 is the share of consumer expenditure on goods other than housing; p is the price index associated with these other goods; and p_h is the price of housing. The prices of other goods are assumed to be determined on national markets, and are therefore exogenous to the region. The parameters b_1 and b_2 reflect the responsiveness of migration to real wages and house prices respectively.

In the housing market, the demand for housing is given by

$$H^d = \alpha + L^s + \beta_1(w - s_0p) - \beta_2p_h \qquad (A2.3)$$

The inclusion of L^s reflects the fact that migration shifts the aggregate demand for housing in the region. Given the size of the population (L^s), housing demand is also influenced by the real income of the population, as reflected in their real wage. The regional supply of housing is given by

$$H^s = \gamma + \delta p_h \qquad (A2.4)$$

Equilibrium in the labour market implies the following relationship between changes in wages and changes in house prices:

$$dw = [b_2/(c+b_1)]dp_h \qquad (A2.5)$$

while equilibrium in the housing market entails that

$$dp_h = [(\beta_1 + b_1)/(\beta_2 + \delta + b_2)]dw \qquad (A2.6)$$

We assume that the dynamics of price (including wage) changes are such that excess demand leads to increases and excess supply to decreases in prices:

$$dp_h/dt = F(H^d - H^s), \text{ where } F' > 0. \qquad (A2.7)$$

$$dw/dt = G(L^d - L^s), \text{ where } G' > 0.$$

On the basis of these dynamics we can derive conditions for stability in regional housing and labour markets. By stability we mean that the markets will respond to any shock, which takes the markets away from equilibrium, by eventually returning to equilibrium. In this model stability requires that

$$(c + b_1)/b_2 > (\beta_1 + b_1)/(\beta_2 + \delta + b_2) \qquad \text{(A2.8)}$$

From (8) it follows that regional housing and labour market stability is more likely

1) the more responsive is migration to wages (higher b_1);
2) the larger the wage elasticity of the demand for labour (c);
3) the lower is the income elasticity of housing demand (β_1);
4) the higher is the price elasticity of housing demand (β_2);
5) the higher is the price elasticity of housing supply (δ);
6) the less responsive is migration to house prices (lower b_2)
   if $(c + b_1)/b_2^2 > (\beta_1 + b_1)/(\delta + b_2 + \beta_2)^2$.

Thus, for instance, an unstable regional economy could result from a combination of low responsiveness of migration to wages, high responsiveness of migration to house prices, a high income elasticity of housing demand and low price elasticities of housing demand and supply.

The analysis of stability can be simplified by noting that the migration responses to nominal (product) wages and house prices are likely to be related, so that $b_2 = kb_1$. For instance, if migration purely responds to *real* wages, then k is the share of housing expenditure in household budgets (perhaps about 0.25). The stability condition (A2.8) can be re-written as

$$c/b_1 > (k\beta_1 - \delta - \beta_2)/(\beta_2 + \delta + kb_1) \qquad \text{(A2.8')}$$

It follows that stability is more likely the smaller is k, and a sufficient condition for stability is that $\delta + \beta_2 > k\beta_1$.

Consider an extreme case in which k=1. Because empirical studies suggest that price and income elasticities of housing demand are roughly equal in magnitude, the sufficient condition would be satisfied as long as housing supply exhibited some price elasticity. For smaller values of k, it is even more likely that the stability condition is satisfied.

If the regional economy is stable, the impacts of demand and supply shifts in one market on price in the other market can be derived. For example, an autonomous increase in the regional housing stock reduces the regional product wage (w), while an exogenous increase in labour demand raises regional house prices. An autonomous increase in regional labour supply, say because of more international migration, may raise or lower house prices, depending on the value of the income elasticity of housing demand relative to the wage elasticity of labour demand; if the former is higher, the increase in labour supply would lower regional house prices. Finally, an upward shift in the demand for housing raises the regional product wage.

Notes

1   Comparisons between the financial risks faced by building societies and the plight of their United States counterparts, the savings and loans, or thrifts, can be misleading. Part of their problems are associated with the contrast between the high interest rates they must pay for deposits and the fixed interest rate mortgages that they hold. But, paradoxically, it has been their diversification away from home mortgages, particularly into commercial property, that has led to the insolvency of many thrifts. Less than half of the assets of the insolvent thrifts are in mortgages, and some have as much as half in commercial property. Deposit insurance (from the Federal Savings and Loan Corporation) has, in effect, underwritten this speculation in commercial property, and the opportunity to sell mortgages on a secondary market (which in large part owes its existence to subsidised default insurance and government guarantees for some of the mortgage–backed securities issued in this market) helped them change their asset portfolio away from mortgages.

2   While, as noted earlier, the fiscal reliefs associated with owner–occupation are partly responsible for the demise of the rental housing market, they are far from being solely responsible.

3   $$OUTSE_t = -112.0 + 0.723*OUTSE_{t-1} + 102.3*RHPSE_t - 64.1\Delta RHPSE_{t-1} \quad (4)$$
     (4.40) (9.54)   (5.34)   (2.07)
     $R^2 = 0.949$ SE=5.13 DW=2.14 Q(3)=0.80 LM=0.08 N=15(1972–86)

     $$INSE_t = 13.21 + 133.2*\Delta RHPSE_t + 98.8*RHPSE_{t-2} \quad (5)$$
     (0.40)   (4.31)   (4.40)

     $R^2 = 0.668$ SE=6.62 DW=2.07 Q(3)=1.33 N=15(1972–86)
     where t indicates year, OUTSE and INSE are out–migration from and in–migration to the south–east respectively, RHPSE is the ratio of the average house price in the south–east to that in the rest of the United Kingdom, and $\Delta X_t = X_t - X_{t-1}$. Q is the Box–Pierce statistic computed over the first three autocorrelations of the residual, and LM is the Lagrange Multiplier statistic for first order autocorrelation, distributed as F(1,9), DW is the Durbin–Watson statistic, and SE is the standard error of the equation. Absolute value of t–statistics are given in parentheses.

4   The national real house price and its first two lags were used as instruments for $\Delta RHPSE_t$ in a Wu test (t=0.19) and in the following two–stage least squares regression:

     $$INSE_t = 7.4 + 130.7*\Delta RHPSE_t + 102.7*RHPSE_{t-2} \quad (5')$$
     (0.13) (2.58)   (2.73)

     $R^2 = 0.666$ SE=6.64 DW=2.03 Q(3)=1.22 N=15(1972–86)

3 The macroeconomic effects of housing market policies under alternative mortgage conditions
Geoffrey Meen

Introduction

There has been a growing recognition in recent years of the importance of interrelationships between housing markets and other markets, whether they be goods, labour or financial. However, conventional United Kingdom macroeconomic models have been slow to recognise this interdependence and housing is generally relegated to a minor role. Simple equations may exist for housing investment and perhaps house prices, but no real attempt is made to fully integrate the housing market into the rest of the model.

Recent statements by the Chancellor suggest that he, at least, believes that the housing market plays a more important role than models would indicate and indeed one of the prime objectives of policy recently has been to reduce the rate of increase in house prices. Since it has traditionally been believed that house prices *respond* to the pressure of demand rather than being a *cause* and the government has actively been promoting the cause of home–ownership since 1980, it is not immediately clear why the Chancellor should be concerned about high house prices (since they have, in themselves, little impact on the RPI), unless he believes that there are further transmission mechanisms by which the housing market affects the real economy and contributes to overheating.

In this chapter we, firstly, attempt to quantify some of the interrelationships that have been suggested as important and, secondly, examine through simulations using the Oxford Economic Forecasting (OEF) model, the potential of housing market policies for reducing the pressure of demand. We do not claim, by any means, that the OEF model covers all the important interactions between housing and other markets – the lack of a regional dimension to the model, in particular, makes this difficult – but the point we wish to stress and which is the central focus of this chapter, is that liberalisation of mortgage markets since the early 1980s has had a dramatic effect on the effectiveness of any policy action. In particular, as we will demonstrate, interest rate policy becomes a much more potent weapon in a deregulated, unrationed mortgage market than in a controlled market.

In recent years unprecedented changes have taken place in the structure of the United Kingdom mortgage market. Among the most important changes, we may list the following:
(i) competition in the mortgage market has increased dramatically in the 1980s. Building societies, as the main providers of housing finance, have faced limited competition in the past, but both United Kingdom and foreign banks in particular now provide large volumes of mortgage funds;
(ii) the increasing use by building societies of term and high interest share accounts to promote competition both between societies and with other financial institutions;
(iii) the relaxation of the taxation provisions relating to building society interest payments, which has allowed societies to raise funds on the wholesale money markets, both in the United Kingdom and abroad;
(iv) the decision by societies to set the interest rate, even on ordinary share accounts, at a level related more closely to market interest rates;
(v) greater provision by building societies of loans not directly for house purchase by their 'traditional' borrowers (for example, loans for home improvements and funds for the purchase of public sector dwellings);
(vi) new legislation concerning the areas in which building societies are permitted to operate came into force in 1987, allowing societies to operate in more diverse areas and to hold a wider range of assets than has traditionally been the case.

The list implies that the mortgage market now bears little relationship to that in existence from the end of the war to the mid–1970s. Whereas the market was dominated by building societies whose main business was to attract funds from households and to lend the majority of funds in the form of mortgages, within a few years we may expect the mortgage market to be multinational in nature and for mortgage institutions to be interested in a far wider range of assets than traditional mortgages.

Interactions between the housing and other markets
In spite of strong fluctuations in private sector housebuilding, the collapse in public sector housebuilding (starts in Great Britain fell to a postwar record low of less than 32,000 in 1987), and a tenure shift between the public and private sectors that has seen the owner–occupancy rate rise from 55 per cent in 1979 to 64 per cent at the end of 1987, the aspect of the housing market that has received most attention from macroeconomists recently is the rise in house prices. In 1987 nominal

prices rose by 17 per cent and peaked at an annual rate of increase of approximately 30 per cent in 1988. Rapidly rising house prices may have a number of macroeconomic consequences.

Firstly, increases in house prices lead to a rise in the value of personal sector wealth which may be used directly to finance consumers' expenditure or act as collateral for a loan. Its importance can be judged by the fact that in 1987 the value of residential buildings accounted for approximately 40 per cent of total personal sector gross wealth. We may note that considerable attention has been paid to the likely effects on consumers' expenditure of the stock market crash in October 1987 although ordinary shares held *directly* by persons only account for 6 per cent of wealth (a much larger proportion is held indirectly through equity in insurance and pension funds). Rather less attention empirically has been paid to the effect of increases in house prices on consumption.

Secondly, the nature of the United Kingdom housing market may be a factor contributing to the failure of wage settlements to respond to high levels of unemployment. Regionally dispersed house prices can cause a segmentation of labour markets, provide disincentive to migration and in areas of high house prices lead to high wage demands as cost–of–living–adjustments.

Finally, rapidly increasing house prices aid the process of equity withdrawal with its consequent effect on consumer demand, since the householder's equity share in a dwelling rises quickly. The presence of a deregulated mortgage market where high loan–to–value ratios are permitted is likely to encourage equity withdrawal. Since mortgage debt accounts for approximately 65 per cent of total personal sector liabilities, any policies aimed at reducing total credit outstanding clearly need to be directed at the mortgage market.

Two questions need to be asked. Firstly, is there any quantitative evidence to support any of the above effects, and secondly, if an association does exist, what are the causes of house price inflation and can policies be devised that influence prices? Furthermore, is the efficacy of any such policies influenced by mortgage market conditions?

The effects of the housing market on the economy – some quantitative evidence

There are currently two ways in which the housing and mortgage markets affect the real economy in the OEF model. Equity withdrawal affects the volume of consumers' expenditure and real house prices influence wage settlements. Each of these is discussed in turn.

Effects on consumers' expenditure

The importance of the real value of wealth stocks in determining consumers' expenditure has long been recognised and most United Kingdom econometric models incorporate wealth, in some form, into their consumption functions. The study by Hendry and Ungern Sternberg (1981) has been particularly influential. In most models, however, the definition of wealth is limited to financial assets, so that revaluations of the market value of the dwelling stock have no direct effect on consumers' expenditure. Given the high proportion of total wealth accounted for by dwellings, this is a difficult conclusion to accept, but perhaps because of the poor quality of data on the market value of dwellings, it appears difficult to identify an effect econometrically. Clearly more research is required in this area.

The OEF model is no different from the mainstream. The model identifies two consumption equations, for non–durables and durables. The first, in the spirit of Hendry and Ungern–Sternberg, makes an allowance only for changes in financial wealth, whereas the second, shown below, also takes into account the effect of equity withdrawal. Variable definitions are given in the appendix to this chapter. The equation originally estimated for the Treasury model and reported in Meen *et al.*(1987), provides one of the main links between the mortgage market and the rest of the economy. Equity withdrawal, which is notoriously difficult to measure (see Drayson, 1985; Holmans, 1986), is proxied by a variable that attempts to capture the extent of rationing in the mortgage market (MRAT). Its derivation is discussed below. The expansion of equity withdrawal coincides with the period in which mortgage markets have been liberalised and mortgage rationing has come to an end. The equation is based on the hypothesis that during periods of mortgage rationing, potential households have to provide a higher deposit than they would otherwise desire, requiring them to run down holdings of financial assets and to reduce purchases of consumption goods. The ending of rationing post–1980 has allowed a rebuilding of asset stocks, both physical and financial, to their desired levels through the process of equity withdrawal.

$$\Delta \ln SDUR_t = \underset{(11.5)}{-0.12098} \ln SDUR_{t-4} \underset{(9.6)}{-0.94958} \underset{(5.5)}{-0.00102} \Delta_2 (PCDOT)_{t-2}$$

$$\underset{(4.4)}{-0.00337} \sum_{i=3}^{4} (MRAT/2)_{t-i} + \underset{(11.4)}{0.19174} \sum_{i=0}^{3} \ln(AY/4)_{t-i} + \underset{(5.3)}{0.02022} \ln\left\{\frac{NFWPE}{PC}\right\}_{t-4}$$

$$\underset{(10.0)}{-0.00189} \sum_{i=0}^{2} [(RS-PCDOT)/3]_{t-i} \underset{(2.9)}{-0.00017} (HP)_t \qquad (1)$$

$R^2=0.88$; DW=1.49; SEE=0.0031; LM: $F_{8,56}=2.08$; Arch: $F_{12,40}=0.42$;
Normality: $\chi_2^2=0.12$; Reset: $F_{3,61}=0.61$; Chow: $F_{13,51}=1.18$

Implied long–run relationship

$$\ln SDUR = -7.849 - 0.0279 \, MRAT + 1.5849 \, \ln AY + 0.1671 \, \ln\left\{\frac{NFWPE}{PC}\right\}$$

$$-0.0156(RS-PCDOT) - 0.00141 \, HP$$

Housing and the National Economy

Average earnings

Important work, suggesting that increasing house prices have been responsible for the failure of United Kingdom wage settlements to decelerate can be found in Bover, Muellbauer and Murphy (1988). The arguments are now well-known and are not repeated here, but two points may be noted. First, their hypotheses are tested in the context of the Layard/Nickell (1986) wage model and have not been tested against alternative models. Second, Muellbauer argues that the effect of regional dispersions in house prices do not simply reflect regional demand pressures, but indicate rigidities in the labour market. The interpretation of their findings is very important for their policy conclusions. If house prices truly influence pay settlements, then policy measures, such as imposing tax neutrality on housing as an asset may, under some circumstances, lead to a moderation in pay settlements. But if house prices are simply an indicator of the pressure of demand (and results below suggest house prices are very sensitive to the pressure of demand), then more general deflationary policies are just as likely to lead to a reduction in earnings as policies aimed specifically at the housing market.

In the absence of a full regional model, determining regional house prices, we cannot adequately incorporate Muellbauer's findings into our model. Hence our aims have been more modest and we have investigated the role that national real house prices may play in determining manufacturing average earnings, using a model related to that of Hall (1986). However, given the controversial nature of the relationship between earnings and house prices, two alternative equations exist in the model.

Two cointegrating equations were estimated and are shown below. The first, which might be considered as fairly conventional, relates average earnings to the RPI, the unemployment rate and a measure of trend productivity. In the second equation, however, real house prices were added to the cointegrating equation, leading to a fall in the coefficient on unemployment to −0.01 and suggesting that unemployment had little independent role to play. Excluding the unemployment term yielded equation (3) and the corresponding second-stage equation is shown as (4).

$$\ln ERMF. = -3.4215 + 1.0033\ \ln RPI - 0.0472\ \ln UNP + 0.8707\ \ln TPMF + RES \quad (2)$$
CRDW=0.85; ADF=−4.31; Estimation period: 1971(1)–1987(3)

$$\ln ERMF = 0.9897\ \ln RPI + 0.6611\ \ln TPMF - 2.5298 + 0.1213\ \ln(PH/RPI) + RES \quad (3)$$
CRDW=0.82; ADF=−4.04

$$\Delta \ln ERMF_t = 0.35557\ \Delta \ln ERMF_{t-1} + 0.0126 - 0.0113Q1 - 0.0176Q3$$
$$(4.1) \qquad\qquad (3.6) \quad (3.8) \qquad (5.7)$$

$$+0.2179 \Delta \ln PH_t + 0.0278 \Delta \ln PROFY_t - 0.3760 \Delta \ln RETRAV_t + 0.2637 \Delta \ln RPI_t$$
$$(4.8) \qquad (1.2) \qquad\qquad (2.8) \qquad\qquad (3.1)$$

$$-0.4495(RES)_{t-1} + \text{incomes policy dummies} \qquad (4)$$
$$(6.6)$$

$R^2 = 0.81$; SEE$=0.0083$; DW$=1.88$; LM:$F_{4,47}=1.22$; Arch:$F_{8,35}=1.52$;

Normality: $\chi_2^2 = 0.51$; Reset: $F_{3,48}=2.49$; Chow: $F_{12,39}=0.50$

As they stand, it is most unlikely that either equation captures the true process of earnings determination. Obvious variables omitted here, but included in the Layard/Nickell model, for example, are any measures of labour market mismatch or union pressure. However, it should be noted that the results are not dependent on the cointegrating approach and very similar results are achieved with more conventional one-stage estimation.

Specifying a full model of earnings behaviour is not the principal object of the exercise. Instead we use *both* equations in simulation analysis to show the comparative effects of policies aimed at the housing market under the two alternative hypotheses concerning earnings determination.

The determinants of house prices

If it is true that the house prices have strong links onto the rest of the economy, then it is important to understand the determinants of house prices. In the last ten years, there have been a large number of studies into these determinants (see, for example, Mayes, 1979; Nellis and Longbottom, 1981; Buckley and Ermisch, 1982; Hendry, 1984). However the equation we concentrate on is a slightly revised version of that given in Meen (1988b).

$$\Delta\ln(PH/PC)_t = -0.5910 - 0.1255\ln(PH/PC)_{t-1} + 0.0445\ln(LIQA/PC)_{t-1}$$
$$\qquad\qquad (1.6)\quad (3.8) \qquad\qquad\qquad (0.9)$$

$$+0.0248\ln(ILLIQ/PC)_{t-1} - 0.0076\Delta(MRAT)_{t-1} - 0.0106(MRAT)_{t-3}$$
$$(1.6)\qquad\qquad\qquad (2.3)\qquad\qquad\qquad (3.3)$$

$$+0.3518\ln(RNY)_t + 0.3088\Delta\ln(RNY)_{t-1} - 0.0058(RBM(1-TAX))_t$$
$$(4.2)\qquad\qquad (3.8)\qquad\qquad\qquad (2.4)$$

$$-0.2262\ln(HAT)_{t-1} + 0.0018(PH^e)_t + \text{seasonals} \qquad (5)$$
$$(2.6)\qquad\qquad (6.7)$$

$R^2 = 0.80$; SEE$=0.0156$; DW$=2.10$; LM:$F_{4,77}=0.41$; Arch: $F_{8,65}=0.73$;

Normality: $\chi_2^2 = 2.97$; Reset: $F_{3,78}=4.25$; Chow:(i) $F_{12,69}=1.01$;

Chow:(ii) $F_{28,53}=1.55$

Implied long-run relationship
$$\ln(PH/PC) = -4.709 + 0.3546\ln(LIQA/PC) + 0.1976\ln(ILLIQ/PC) - 0.0845(MRAT)$$
$$+2.803\ln(RNY) - 0.0462(RBM(1-TAX)) - 1.8024\ln(HAT)$$

The underlying theory of the equation is described in detail in Meen (1988b), but it specifies real second–hand house prices (PH/PC) as a function of real per capita income (RNY), the nominal post–tax mortgage interest rate (RBM(1–TAX)), the extent of mortgage rationing (MRAT), real wealth (ILLIQ/PC and LIQA/PC), the ratio of the owner–occupied dwelling stock to the number of households (HAT) and expected capital gains on housing (PH^e). The equation is well–determined statistically and is not rejected by any of the diagnostic statistics with the exception of the RESET test. Two post–sample Chow tests are presented, the first covering the period 1985(1)–1987(4) and the second the period 1981(1)–1987(4). Stability is not rejected by either.

Most of the determinants of house prices given in equation (5) are common ground in the studies mentioned above. Income is almost always a highly important determinant, with a long–run elasticity of 2.8 in equation (5), showing why concentration on house price to earnings ratios has, in the past, proved a popular rule–of–thumb for predicting future house price movements. However, as equation (5) indicates, the determinants are more complex and for reasons discussed later, price/earnings ratios are now less likely to provide an adequate guide to future house price changes.

The distinctive feature of equation (5) is its treatment of housing/mortgage market interactions. The potential importance of a shortage of mortgage funds for the housing market has long been recognised. In the late 1950s and early 1960s, fluctuations in the availability of mortgage credit were cited as the principal explanation of counter–cyclical movements in United States residential construction during the postwar period (for example, Schaaf, 1958). Graphically a close relationship between the volume of construction output and the level of mortgage lending has been demonstrated by Guttentag (1961) and Alberts (1962) in the United States, by Gough (1975) and Vipond (1969) in the United Kingdom and by Fischer and Siegman (1972) for a number of countries.

However, empirical testing of the relationship between the mortgage and housing markets is not straightforward. With one or two exceptions, measures of mortgage rationing incorporated into housing market studies may be categorised in three ways: (a) measures of the spread between mortgage interest rates and market rates; (b) measures of deposit inflows into the main mortgage lending institutions; and (c) measures based on the mortgage stock or net mortgage advances.

Proxy measures such as these, however, are unsatisfactory when there are fundamental shifts in the mortgage market such as we have experienced in the United Kingdom in the 1980s. For example, if the mortgage stock is used as a measure of rationing and building society policy changes so that rationing no longer exists, how do we modify the housing price equation to cope with the change? A related criticism is made by Fair (1972). The mortgage market will have a constraining effect on housing activity if excess mortgage demand occurs, but in general excess supply will have no effect, so that an asymmetry arises between conditions of excess demand and supply. Few studies adequately cope with this asymmetry. Finally we may note that the mortgage stock is invalid as a regressor in periods of excess mortgage supply and its use will give rise to simultaneous equation bias.

In principle, the estimation of models usually labelled as 'disequilibrium models' provides an alternative to the use of proxy measures for mortgage rationing. Indeed, beginning with the Fair and Jaffee (1972), which proposed a model of mortgage rationing to examine the impact on the level of housing starts, disequilibrium modelling techniques have proved popular in the housing literature. Although we do not wish to discuss these techniques in detail, disequilibrium modelling techniques still appear to suffer from a number of problems. The underlying models of the housing market have remained generally simple in terms of structure, choice of regressors and the treatment of model dynamics (for recent models see, for example, Markandya and Pemberton, 1984 and Askari, 1986). In fact, it is still a feature of most econometric models of the housing market that models that are relatively realistic in analysing the housing market as a whole are ad hoc in their treatment of disequilibrium, whilst those that employ more complex methods in their treatment of disequilibrium tend to be less realistic.

Our own measure of the influence of the mortgage market on house prices avoids some of the problems. Mortgage market effects are measured by MRAT – the degree of excess demand in the mortgage market. In periods of excess supply (which have been the majority since 1981), the variable takes a value of zero. The derivation of the rationing indicator is described in detail in Meen (1985). However in summary, MRAT is measured as the difference between estimated mortgage demand and supply. The supply equation is based on the ideas in Anderson and Hendry (1984). In this study building societies face a cost function which they wish to minimise. The arguments in the cost function are diverse, reflecting a multiplicity of objectives, but one of these objectives is to meet the volume of mortgages demanded by households. The conflict with alternative objectives means that rationing takes place, but mortgage supply still responds positively to expected mortgage demand. Expected mortgage demand is related positively to house prices and income and negatively to the mortgage rate. An implication, perhaps contrary to expectations, is that mortgage supply is, therefore, *negatively* related to the mortgage interest rate.

The income, house price and interest rate terms are highly significant in estimation and it can be shown, under certain circumstances, that even if periods of excess supply are never observed, the parameters of the implied mortgage demand function can be identified from the estimated supply equation. Expected mortgage demand is then subtracted from mortgage supply to measure the extent of rationing.

The influence of MRAT, as can be seen from equation (5), is well determined empirically both in differences and in levels. Furthermore from the way it is specified, we can examine the impact of housing market policies under alternative mortgage regimes – the period of rationing up to 1980 and the unrationed period since 1980. Also by modelling both the housing and mortgage markets, both the direct effect of any policy change on housing and any indirect effects working through the mortgage market and influencing the extent of rationing can be taken into account. To take an example, any change to the tax treatment of housing which changes the effective mortgage rate, will affect house prices directly and also indirectly by changing the demand for mortgages, since as mentioned above, mortgage demand is negatively related to the mortgage rate.

Housing market policies

The tax treatment of owner–occupied housing has become the bête–noire of many housing economists. A number of authors have been concerned with the relative returns to housing and competing assets, with a non–neutral tax system particularly under inflationary conditions (see, for example, Ebrill and Possen, 1982; Hendershott and Hu, 1981; Summers, 1981; Kau and Keenan, 1983). These studies all indicate that tax non–neutrality leads to a rise in the relative return to housing and consequently to an increase in the real asset price. Bover, Muellbauer and Murphy (1988) also suggest reform of the housing tax system as a means of moderating house price rises and hence influencing labour markets and the volume of consumers' expenditure.

In this section we evaluate these proposals. We attempt to show that even if house price rises have been a factor in the overheating of the United Kingdom economy, it does not *necessarily* imply that the cause has been the tax distortions in favour of owner–occupied housing. This depends on mortgage market conditions.

We consider four scenarios: (1) rationing exists in the mortgage market; earnings are influenced by house prices; (2) no rationing exists; earnings are affected by house prices; (3) rationing exists in the mortgage market; earnings are not affected by house prices; (4) no rationing exists; earnings are not affected by house prices.

A number of different measures have been proposed for removing tax distortions – abolition of mortgage tax relief (MTR), taxation of capital gains on owner–occupied dwellings, taxes on imputed rental incomes. We have chosen to examine the former, although the essential points also hold for the remaining options (and indeed, are also applicable to an analysis of the imposition of the poll tax). We might also note that in general terms, most of the results apply to interest rate policies as a whole, and are not restricted to measures aimed at the housing market.

For each of the four scenarios, full simulations on the OEF model are carried out over the period 1982(1)–1986(4). The absolute values of our results are dependent on the base used; where this is particularly important, it is indicated. However, the relative results of each scenario are not base dependent.

Two assumptions are required. Firstly, given the large sums spent on mortgage tax relief, its abolition in the absence of other changes would impart a strong deflationary bias into the economy as personal sector disposable incomes fell. To offset this we could make one of two conventional assumptions; we might assume a fixed money target, so that as the PSBR fell government debt sales were reduced, implying a reduction in interest rates. Hence any deflationary fall in real incomes is at least partly offset by the reflationary impact of a fall in interest rates. Alternatively, we might assume that MTR abolition is ex ante revenue–neutral, so that the increased tax yield is given back in the form of other income tax cuts. We have chosen the latter option.

The second assumption concerns how the housing finance institutions respond to the abolition of mortgage tax relief. In Meen (1988a), it was shown that the effect of MTR abolition on house prices depends, particularly when no mortgage rationing is present, on:
(i) The interest rate elasticity of the deposits of the mortgage finance institutions. If the interest rate elasticity is zero, institutions can offset any effects on the housing market by reducing the mortgage rate (so that the post–tax rate returns to its former level). Given a fixed relationship between the mortgage rate and the deposit rate, the deposit rate would also be reduced, but with a zero interest rate elasticity, there would be no loss of deposits. However, at the opposite extreme, if the interest rate elasticity of deposits is infinite, mortgage institutions cannot offset any effects on the housing market from MTR abolition, since any attempt at reducing their own rates would lead to a complete loss of deposits.
(ii) The interest rate responses of those institutions competing with mortgage finance organisations for funds. In this case even if interest rate deposit elasticities are high, this becomes irrelevant if all competing organisations reduce their deposit rates in line with each other.

The equations for personal sector asset demands in the model, in fact, suggest that asset substitutability is high (for example, the long–run interest rate semi–elasticity for building society deposits is 0.15). Also it seems unlikely that MTR abolition would lead to a large general reduction in interest rates. Both of these factors suggest that there would be little scope for the mortgage institutions to cut their own interest rates and offset the housing market effects of MTR abolition. Therefore we have assumed no change in mortgage rates.

Results from the four scenarios are shown in tables 3.1–3.4. The first two tables deal with the case where house prices have a direct impact on average earnings, that is, they use equation (4). Tables 3.3 and 3.4 use the alternative earnings equation where unemployment replaces the house price terms. Tables 3.1 and 3.3 each present two sets of results; we demonstrated above that one of the main ways in the model in which the mortgage market affects the rest of the economy is through equity withdrawal and its influence on consumers' expenditure. We have separated this effect from the remaining effects of MTR abolition on the economy. Therefore the figures in table 3.1a show the effect of abolishing mortgage tax relief, abstracting from the effect of changes in equity withdrawal, whereas the figures in table 3.1b show the total results. One reason for making the distinction is that abolition of MTR

Table 3.1a Rationed mortgage markets; house prices *affect* earnings (no equity withdrawal effect)

% change from base except where otherwise specified

Year	House prices	Investment in dwellings	GDP	Consumers' expenditure	RPI	Average earnings	Current account (£m)
1	−5.8	−1.4	0.1	0.1	1.2	0.0	0
2	−11.0	−3.9	−0.3	−0.3	1.0	−0.7	320
3	−8.9	−3.9	−0.4	−0.5	1.0	−0.1	540
4	−6.5	−2.8	−0.2	−0.1	1.5	0.7	70
5	−6.0	−2.6	−0.1	0.1	1.8	1.0	−120

Table 3.1b Rationed mortgage markets; house prices *affect* earnings (full effects)

1	−5.7	−1.4	0.0	0.2	1.2	−0.01	−30
2	−10.9	−3.8	0.1	0.3	1.0	−0.6	−90
3	−8.6	−3.7	0.1	0.4	1.2	0.1	−190
4	−6.4	−2.8	0.2	0.7	1.8	1.0	−480
5	−6.4	−2.8	0.2	0.7	2.2	1.2	−430

Table 3.2 Unrationed mortgage market; house price *affect* earnings

1	−6.8	−1.6	0.0	0.1	1.2	−0.2	20
2	−16.6	−5.5	−0.5	−0.6	0.8	−1.7	560
3	−21.1	−7.8	−1.0	−1.4	0.0	−2.6	1410
4	−22.6	−8.5	−1.1	−1.6	−0.5	−3.0	1390
5	−23.0	−8.6	−1.0	−1.6	−1.1	−3.5	1180

Table 3.3a Rationed mortgage markets; house prices *do not* affect earnings (no equity withdrawal effect)

1	−5.6	−1.4	0.0	0.2	1.2	0.7	−90
2	−9.4	−3.9	0.0	0.4	1.8	2.0	−70
3	−6.3	−3.6	−0.2	0.2	2.7	2.9	250
4	−4.6	−2.8	−0.2	0.3	3.4	3.6	300
5	−3.8	−2.7	−0.1	0.4	3.7	4.0	90

Table 3.3b Rationed mortgage markets; house prices *do not* affect earnings (full effect)

1	−5.6	−1.4	0.1	0.3	1.2	0.7	−120
2	−9.2	−3.9	0.4	1.0	1.8	2.2	−490
3	−5.9	−3.5	0.4	1.1	3.0	3.2	−490
4	−4.3	−2.8	0.2	1.0	3.9	4.1	−190
5	−4.0	−2.9	0.2	1.1	4.3	4.6	−270

Table 3.4   Unrationed mortgage markets; house prices *do not affect* earnings

Year	House prices	Invest– ment in dwellings	GDP	Consumers' expendi– ture	RPI	Average earnings	Current account (£m)
1	−6.6	−1.6	0.0	0.2	1.2	0.7	−80
2	−14.6	−5.5	−0.1	0.3	1.7	1.9	60
3	−17.0	−7.4	−0.5	−0.2	2.6	2.6	790
4	−17.5	−7.9	−0.8	−0.6	3.1	3.1	1240
5	−17.4	−8.0	−0.9	−0.6	3.1	3.2	1150

leads to a reduction in mortgage rationing in the model as the demand for mortgages falls.   In principle, this implies that for those households who still wish to take out mortgages, the loan to value ratio can potentially rise and households have to find a smaller deposit, allowing a higher level of financial assets and consumption.   However the real interest rate used in equation (1) is not the real post–tax mortgage rate which has risen, but a more general interest rate which is unchanged by assumption.   Therefore the effect on consumers' expenditure of MTR abolition is likely to be overstated.

Since our main interest is to show how the results vary according to mortgage market conditions, tables 3.2 and 3.4 also abstract from the equity withdrawal effect.

The rationed case
From equation (5), if rationing in the mortgage market exists, we expect two effects on house prices from MTR abolition: (i) a negative direct effect as the post–tax mortgage rate rises; (ii) a positive indirect effect as the degree of mortgage rationing falls.

A priori, the total effect is unknown.   The cost of funds to those who already have mortgage rises, but any effective rationing constraints, has a shadow price associated with it and any relaxation of the constraint means that the cost of capital to those previously rationed out of the market may actually fall.   The theoretical analysis can be found in Meen (1988).   Table 3.1a suggests that, abstracting from equity withdrawal effects, house prices fall by approximately 6 per cent in the long run when earnings are affected by house prices.   In the case where earnings are unaffected (table 3.3a) the effect is less than 4 per cent. It should be pointed out, however, that this is a case where the results are base dependent.   Over the simulation period, mortgage rationing was, in fact, absent (1982–6), but Meen (1988a) shows that when a related simulation is carried out over the period 1974–9 (when rationing was present), the long-run effect on house prices is approximately zero.   It

39

may also be noticed that the short–run effects on house prices are greater than the long–run effects; this is because equation (5) suggests that households react more quickly to changes in the mortgage rate than to changes in the extent of rationing. Tables 3.1 and 3.3 both show small negative effects on GDP, but the effects on the RPI on average earnings are very different according to which earnings equation is employed. In table 3.1 earnings rise by less than the RPI (since house prices have fallen) and the effects on both are relatively small. In table 3.3, however, earnings and prices both rise strongly and are approximately 4 per cent higher than in the base at the end of the period. In neither of the cases is there much improvement in the current account of the balance of payments.

The unrationed case
The results of the abolition of MTR in the rationed case are shown in tables 3.2 and 3.4. We find that the choice of mortgage regime has important effects on the level of house prices, since by definition MRAT cannot now change to offset the increase in the post–tax mortgage rate. Results again differ accordingly to the choice of earnings equation. In the long run, house prices fall by 23 per cent in the most extreme case and housing investment falls by more than 8 per cent. (We should note that none of the results are truly long–run because changes in the stock of dwellings brought about by changes in investment are not allowed to affect house prices). In table 3.2 the fall in house prices drives a wedge between average earnings and the RPI, average earnings falling by 3.5 per cent in the final year. The reduction in real earnings leads to a fall in consumers' expenditure and GDP which is approximately 1 per cent lower than in the base. The reduction in domestic demand also leads to a substantial improvement in the current account balance. In table 3.4, the fall in house prices is still substantial (17.5 per cent), but as expected, the main difference from table 3.2 is that the rduction in average earnings no longer takes place.

Policy conclusions
The model strongly suggests that conditions in the mortgage market are of crucial importance to the effectiveness of any policy action aimed specifically at the housing market. It also indicates that looking at the housing market alone can lead to incorrect policy conclusions. At one extreme, in the rationed case, tax changes aimed at imposing neutrality between housing and other assets may have negligible effects on house prices and the economy at large. One implication of this is that past inflation of house prices during rationed periods cannot be blamed on the existence of tax incentives to owner–occupiers. It also follows that even if average earnings are responsive to movements in house prices, high levels of wage settlements in previous decades are not attributable to the tax treatment of owner–occupation.

In the liberalised conditions of today, the analysis suggests that house prices would be strongly affected by policies aimed directly at the housing market, such as MTR abolition, although the results hold for a wider range of policies such as increases in interest rates. Particularly if average earnings are influenced by house prices, such actions would lead to lower house prices, consumer demand, prices and earnings and a substantial improvement in the current balance (note however that the precise numbers for the change in the current balance are base dependent). Furthermore, these results are formulated under the assumption of revenue neutrality, which might make the idea of the reform of housing market finance slightly more palatable. Such a change might be considered a high risk strategy, however. The idea that changes in house prices affect average earnings is relatively new and more research is probably needed. The possibility of a fall in house prices (although the model only suggests a deceleration of the rate of increase) is not likely to be politically popular and indeed, in another paper (Meen, 1988a) it was argued that the time to remove mortgage tax relief would have been during the rationed period, when effects on property values would have been minimised.

As mentioned earlier, the model makes no claim to incorporate all the possible links between the housing market and the rest of the economy. The tables suggest, under rationing, that increasing equity withdrawal might offset some of the deflationary impact of MTR abolition on consumers' expenditure, although we pointed out that the interest rate effects on consumers' expenditure might be misspecified in these circumstances. Potentially a reduced market value of the housing stock could cause wealth effects that reduce consumers' expenditure further. More research is required to identify whether such effects exists. However, we may note again, that the importance of such effects will depend on the mortgage regime in operation.

We can now see why current house price/earnings ratios are no longer likely to provide a good guide to future price trends. From equation (5), the main determinants of house prices are found to be real income, the post–tax mortgage rate and the measure of rationing. In rationed periods, the equation suggests that the effect on prices of any changes in the mortgage rate will be at least partly offset by changes in the extent of rationing. Hence the total effect of changes in the mortgage rate is small and for the past, the prices/earnings ratio probably provided a reasonable guide to price movements in the long run. However, in today's conditions the equation implies that prices have become much more interest elastic and price predictions cannot be made even in the long run, without taking into account the mortgage rate. If the mortgage rate is low, for example, this is perfectly consistent with a continuing high price/earnings ratio.

Clearly the point of liberalising the mortgage market was not to increase the effectiveness of policy instruments aimed at the housing market, but that has been the result, since the mortgage market no longer acts as a buffer to housing market policies. The existence of tax advantages to owner–occupation, introduced during periods of rationing, is unlikely to have been the cause of house price increases and we should be wary of ascribing all the ills of the housing market to tax non–neutrality, but the freeing up of mortgage markets during the 1980s has made housing policy potentially a more important instrument.

Appendix

AY	Personal sector 'inflation–adjusted' real disposable income (£m constant prices)
ERMF	Manufacturing average earnings (1980=100)
HAT	Ratio of the stock of owner–occupied dwellings to the number of houses (%).
HP	Minimum downpayment percentage for hire purchase (%)
ILLIQ	Personal sector 'illiquid' financial assets (£mn)
LIQA	Personal sector 'liquid' financial assets (£mn)
MRAT	Measure of mortgage market rationing (%)
NFWPE	Personal sector net financial wealth (£m)
PC	Consumers' expenditure deflator (1980=1.0)
PCDOT	Annual rate of inflation ($100*\Delta_4 \ln PC$)
PH	D.O.E/B.S.A Index of mix–adjusted second–hand house prices (1980=100)
PH^e	'Expected' rate of increase of house prices ($200*\Delta_2 \ln PH_{t-1}$)
PROFY	Non–North Sea post–tax company profits per unit of output (%)
Q1,Q3	Quarterly seasonal dummies
RBM	Average building society mortgage interest rate (%)
RES	Equation residual
RETRAV	Personal sector retained earnings as a percentage of wages and salaries (%)
RNY	Per capita personal sector real disposable income (£m)
RPI	Retail prices index (Jan 1987=100)
RS	3 month interbank deposit rate (%)
SDUR	Stock of consumer durable goods (£m constant prices)
TAX	Basic rate of income tax (%)
TPMF	Measure of trend productivity in manufacturing (1980=100)
UNP	Unemployment rate (%)
R^2	Coefficient of determination
SEE	Equation standard error
DW	Durbin–Watson statistics for 1st order autocorrelation
LM	Lagrange Multiplier test for 4th order autocorrelation
Arch	Engle's ARCH test for heteroscedasticity
Normality	Jarque and Bera's test statistic for normally distributed errors
Reset	Ramsey's 'Reset' test
Chow	Chow's post–sample test of prediction errors
CRDW	Cointegrating equation Durbin–Watson statistic
DF	Dickey–Fuller test statistic
ADF	Augmented Dickey–Fuller test statistic

In addition under each coefficient in the equation, the associated t–value is given.

Comment on Chapter 3

D.N.F. Bell

The main concern of this chapter is with the links between the housing market and the rest of the national economy. The transmission mechanisms which link housing to the rest of the economy have been largely ignored in conventional United Kingdom macroeconomic models. This is inevitable given that the housing sector in these models generally comprises reduced form equations for house prices and housing investment. While Meen does not attempt to construct a structural housing market model, he does draw our attention to the importance of certain key equations both for the housing market and the whole economy.

The macroeconomic consequences of rising house prices might be pervasive. The most obvious such consequence is the wealth effect resulting from the revaluation of an asset which comprises 40 per cent of total personal sector gross wealth. Substantial changes in the price of one asset will inevitably affect the prices at which individuals are prepared to trade other assets. Thus, higher house prices may lead individuals to divest themselves of assets to finance additional consumption thus exerting a downward pressure on, for example, equity prices. This possibility is not directly addressed in this chapter given its orientation toward income, rather than substitution, effects. It is the sort of macroeconomic issue, however, over which Feldstein and Hendershott and Hu have expressed concern.

The failure of the housing market to support the levels of migration necessary to equilibrate regional unemployment rates is a problem mentioned by Meen which is taken up subsequently by Gordon (Chapter 5) and Hughes and McCormick (Chapter 6), who note that 'the amount of migration which can be genuinely attributed to differences in labour market conditions is negligible in relation to the overall magnitude of unemployment differentials'. Meen does not, however, carry this issue forward to econometric work primarily because of the lack of any significant regional component in existing macroeconomic models.

The chapter concentrates on three empirical relationships which link the housing market to the rest of the economy. The first of these is the demand for durable goods. An attempt is made to capture the effects of equity withdrawal on the purchases of durables through a measure of mortgage rationing. When mortgages are rationed, individuals must run down liquid assets to meet higher deposit requirements and so reduce durable purchases. But why stop at durable purchases? The most recent National Institute model includes a general consumption equation where, if individuals are constrained in the credit market, their demand for *all* types of goods is affected.

The second relationship concerns the determination of average earnings. The key issue is whether house prices directly affect wage demands or whether house prices merely reflect the pressure of demand.

With a somewhat different specification from the standard Layard–Nickell model, Meen argues that unemployment and house prices appear to substitute quite well for each other in an equation for manufacturing earnings. From this evidence, it is difficult to conclude unequivocally that house prices play a key role in wage bargaining. Perhaps this issue can only be resolved by investigations at the micro level.

The final relationship concerns the determination of house prices. The innovation in this relationship is principally the variable used to measure the effects of mortgage rationing on house prices. If the supply of credit is not adequate to meet demand, some rationing occurs: if the supply exceeds demand, then rationing will be absent. Rationing occurred principally prior to 1980. The variable is based on the argument that building societies have had a number of objectives, only one of which was the satisfaction of mortgage demand. While this mechanism does provide a potentially important link between the credit and housing markets, the present situation is characterised by excess mortgage supply, which means that the two markets have become 'unhitched', at least through mortgage rationing. Thus, the influence of the rest of the economy on house prices must come from other sources, notably through the determination of real income, interest rates and assets, both liquid and illiquid.

The remainder of the chapter deals with simulations of the effects of the removal of mortgage tax relief using the Oxford Economic Forecasting model which utilises some of the relationships already discussed. Not surprisingly, the results are sensitive to the assumptions made about the state of rationing in the mortgage market. For the foreseeable future, it seems reasonable to assume that such rationing will not exist in the United Kingdom. Without the restraining influence which rationing provides, the model indicates quite large impacts on house prices, house–building and major macro–aggregates, particularly if the hypothesis that house prices affect earnings is accepted.

These kinds of simulation provide a useful first attempt to calibrate the links between the housing sector and the macroeconomy. This area of interaction between the housing market, the labour market and the rest of the economy has hardly begun to be explored though it is now recognised as being relevant to many current macroeconomic problems. Meen has done a valuable service in beginning to research this area.

Comment on International Comparisons of Macroeconomic Effects
(based on a conference paper by Robert Buckley and Stephen Mayo of the
World Bank)

Michael Dicks

The main conclusion of their paper is that off–budget considerations can
be more important than on–budget spending (that is, implicit subsidies or
taxes can be 'big'). This suggests that if we are to analyse policy then
we need to look at regulatory frameworks, pricing policies and financial
policies (especially developments in the credit market). The latter is
particularly important since housing has a big impact on the rest of the
economy – including labour markets and households' consumption/savings
decisions.

Their analysis of *Polish* housing and labour markets suggest some
features in common with the United Kingdom, though few and rather more
extreme. Firstly, the authors make the point that interest rates are set
by the Polish government and are far too low, for example, –48 per cent.
Secondly, there are big subsidies to housing, both direct and indirect.
As regards the United Kingdom, there are few direct subsidies but there
were indirect subsidies in the 1970s, with building societies trying to
keep interest rate levels and variability low. Indeed, one might argue
that there are still some very slight forms of rationing. Thirdly, both
contries have *price controls*; thus state rents are low. In the United
Kingdom, of course, this policy has to some extent been offset in recent
years by the move to raise public sector rents more closely in line with
market rents. At the same time, however, sales of public sector housing
have also been at knock–down prices, thus introducing a new, if
temporary, subsidy.

Three main *macro–housing linkages* arise in their analysis. All are
relevant to the United Kingdom. First, Poland clearly has an acute
housing shortage (the number of households far exceeding the number of
dwellings), whereas in the United Kingdom we only have a small problem
and much of this is due to where the existing stock is located. The
result of this shortage is that potential rates of return from investment
in housing are very high in Poland. We need to ask if this is also the
case in the United Kingdom. Profitability of private housebuilding does
seem high currently (as the accounts of some of the main United Kingdom
housebuilders indicate), but they are mainly accounted for by capital
gains on land. This highlights one of the problems in the United
Kingdom; little land is made available. This implies that its price is
bid up and quantity remains broadly unchanged; that is, our housing
shortage is not only much less severe, but it depends to a large degree
upon what one might call environmental issues such as how planning
permission should be granted, who should have a say and whether or not
side payments should be allowed and so on.

The second main topic in common between the countries is labour
mobility (see also Chapter 2). In Poland it is clear that there are not

enough houses, hence people hold on to them. Surely there are also parallels here. For example, it is easy to look at changes in regional house prices and say, 'there is a problem' (people want to move south but cannot), but the trouble is one cannot move the houses to where they are needed. Therefore, ultimately, one must build more or convert existing dwellings.

There are various possible answers to the United Kingdom problem. As Ermisch points out in Chapter 2, we could wait; eventually, if wages and house prices respond differently in different regions, new equilibrium house price earnings ratios will emerge. Another answer would be for firms to move, but this has largely been ignored. We could try and ensure greater supply response in housing in the south; that is, make it easier to build houses and more profitable to do so. Is it the case that, at the moment, house prices bid up land prices very quickly, causing capital gains for existing landowners, but little quantity response even in the long run? Are there still not enough houses in the south? Given the sensitivity of aggregate housing starts to economic conditions, this is the big question (see, for example, NEDO forecasts which show 205,000 housing starts in 1988 and 165,000 in 1989). Finally, if one believes that council tenants are less mobile than owner–occupiers, rent subsidies could be either ended or reduced and the houses sold cheaply instead. Given that this is already being done to some extent in the United Kingdom, has it been effective?

Savings

Poland generally has had negative rates of return which leads the authors to claim that many households adopt the 'consume all income' approach. In the United Kingdom, real rates are now high and fairly stable, implying that one would expect a 'high' saving ratio. In recent years, though, the saving ratio has fallen (and more quickly than one might expect given changes in income and so on). The fall could have been caused by, first, wealth effects/equity withdrawal (note that there may be some adjustment to new equilibrium *still* going on). People can realise past capital gains more easily. Second, lower inflation implies lower precautionary/transactions savings. Also the reduction in liquidity constraints means that households need not save up for deposits to the same extent as they used to. Third, confidence might be higher. This could be because liquidity constraints have been reduced. A distinction needs to be drawn between permanent and current income, with more households now being able to smooth consumption over the life–cycle. It may also be due to greater confidence in future real earnings growth because of the Government's commitment to reducing inflation. Fourth, the fall could have been caused by data problems. The gap between the traditional measure of savings (that is, the difference between income and consumption) and that suggested by changes in the personal sector balance sheet has grown enormously in recent years. Income may be seriously under–recorded – in which case the saving ratio could really be around 8–12 per cent.

Certainly it is the case that we have moved from a position of *some* rationing to one of much less, although one might argue that some rationing still exists (one cannot, for example, have an index–linked mortgage). This has *not*, however, stimulated savings (despite the high interest elasticity suggested by the estimates of a non–durables equation in my recent paper (see Dicks, 1988b).

All in all then, many of the problems which Poland would face were it to encourage competition in the mortgage and housing markets are similar (though of much greater magnitude) to those which have occurred in the United Kingdom in the 1980s as the Government has reduced subsidies, sold off council houses, encouraged competition in the mortgage market and brought greater price stability (and a declining inflation rate). Here it has given rise to greater housing investment (but note that much of this has been in improvements). It has also had (probably small) effects on labour mobility and (possibly large effects on) personal sector consumption/savings decisions although here the econometric evidence is very weak. The main problem in the United Kingdom is that policy has helped to give an (unexpected) boost to demand which elicited little supply response. This highlights the fact that changes in planning regulations (that is, supply–side policies) need to go hand–in–hand with policies which raise the demand for housing.

Finally, it is worth mentioning dynamics. It is not clear to me that savings rates have, in the short term, been raised (that is, fewer or weaker constraints raise perceptions of long–run/permanent income and therefore increase spending). Here the real question is whether or not this increase in consumption is merely a *temporary* factor. If it is, then will the savings ratio perhaps soon begin to rise?

4 The housing market and and the UK economy: problems and opportunities

John Muellbauer

Introduction[1]

The 1980s have seen dramatic changes in financial markets in general and housing markets in particular. Exchange controls were abolished in the Autumn of 1979. The 'corset' on clearing banks which had restrained the growth and development of wholesale money markets in 1974–80 was removed. In 1981 the clearing banks began aggressively to expand their mortgage lending. As Goodhart (1986) puts it, 'Prior to 1981/82 the limited, and rationed, availability of mortgages meant that the existence of a huge hoard of excellent personal sector collateral, in the form of unencumbered house values, went unutilised, while personal sector borrowing in other forms was relatively expensive and unattractive'. The

Empirical research that forms part of the background for this research was financed under ESRC grant B00220012. Olympia Bover, David Hendry and Anthony Murphy were my research collaborators for different phases of this project. Their contribution has been magnificent and they should not be blamed for errors of interpretation. I am grateful to Richard Layard, Sam Brittan, John Ermisch, John Flemming, Alan Holmans, Gordon Hughes, Mervyn King, Patrick Minford, Stephen Nickell, Mark Robson, Maurice Scott, Peter Spencer and John Vickers for helpful discussions.

Early versions of some of the arguments appeared in the Financial Times *of 23 October and 23 December, 1986. I am grateful to Giles Keating and the other correspondents for their reactions. Responsibility for the views expressed here is mine alone.*

ending of mortgage rationing led to a large rise in the personal sector's debt to income ratio and the phenomenon of mortgage cash withdrawal or 'equity withdrawal' from the housing market. A significant part of the phenomenal rise in the ratio of average United Kingdom house prices to income up to 1988 is explicable by this credit expansion. The forthcoming abolition of domestic rates sustains a substantially higher level of the house price/income ratio than has prevailed in the past. Background information on long–term movements in house and land prices relative to wages or income, and on equity withdrawal, can be found in charts 4.1–4.3.

In the following section the consequences for consumer expenditure of the partial elimination of credit rationing and the wealth effects of the increase in house prices is discussed. Much of the explanation for the decline of the personal sector savings rate in the 1980s and the boom in consumer imports is to be found here. These factors account for much of the 1988 trade deficit which has only been exceeded as a share of GDP in 1974. Then the oil shock and miners strike caused a massive short–term jump in Britain's expenditure on imports.

There can be little doubt that there is still a major problem with the supply side of the United Kingdom economy. This is so despite the apparent curbing of the power of trade unions and the achievement from 1981 of a more rapid underlying rate of productivity growth in manufacturing than had been achieved since 1973 (see Muellbauer, 1986). Among the symptoms of this problem are the following: (i) the fact that underlying annual earnings growth in manufacturing (where the figures are less affected by increases in the proportion of female part–time workers) has hovered between 7.75 and 9.5 per cent since 1983 despite high rates of unemployment, which were increasing until Autumn 1986, and a falling rate of retail price inflation; (ii) the fact that the level of vacancies increased by 45 per cent from 1983 Q4 to 1986 Q4 when unemployment continued to grow;[2] (iii) the skill shortages reported in surveys; for example, already in 1986 a European Commission survey found 15 per cent of United Kingdom firms reporting skill shortages while only 4 per cent of German firms did so, despite the lower rates of unemployment experienced in Germany.

Shortages of skilled workers have intensified and appear to be a problem at the national level as well as in the south–east. In parts of the south–east, the most recent survey from the Chambers of Commerce suggests that there is now a generalised staff shortage. Many special location allowances for London and the south–east have leapt since mid–1987 so that the median London allowance for non–manuals at the end of 1988 was £2,250,[3] while staff turnover in the south–east has increased sharply.[4]

Clearly, a national shortage of skilled workers has much more to do with lack of training both in the private sector and in the public sector in the last ten years than with regional mismatch. The Autumn 1988 issue of the *Oxford Review of Economic Policy* examines the training problem in depth. The Director of the Training Commission summarises the position thus: 'At every level we are towards the bottom of the training league table, whether in education, youth training, higher level skills training, or management training'. Clearly, these failures are part of the United Kingdom's continuing supply–side problem. However, drawing on work with Bover and Murphy, it is argued later in this chapter that parts of the problem with the supply side have their roots in distortions in the United Kingdom's housing markets.

The traditional view is that restrictions on the way council housing is allocated and restrictions on tenure and rents in the private rental market which help to account for the decline in that sector have restricted labour mobility. This has led to higher unemployment than would otherwise have existed (see Minford, Ashton and Peel, 1987, and Hughes and McCormick, 1987). We do not argue with this view but suggest that, *in addition*, widening house price differentials between regions of high labour demand and those of low labour demand have restricted mobility and so added to wage pressure for the economy as a whole. These widening house price differentials have been partly caused by an increased demand for housing in the south–east, not for living space but for portfolio investment reasons. Such a demand increase can crowd out workers, especially perhaps manual workers, from the south–east. Lack of mobility suggests a high degree of mismatch in the labour market: high unemployment in one area can coexist with a high level of unfilled vacancies in another if workers fail to move.

These supply–side and demand–side problems are not entirely independent of course. For example, higher real wage increases than would otherwise have occurred have contributed to the growth of consumer expenditure. In turn, there are feedbacks from wages to house prices and, unless effectively resisted by policy, from weakness in the exchange rate resulting from balance of payments deficits back to other prices and to wages. The policy response of high interest rates, in turn, risks the curtailment of investment and the expansion of the United Kingdom's supply–side potential.

The fourth section deals with policy issues. Recent government decisions include the forthcoming abolition of domestic rates and their replacement by the Community Charge or Poll Tax and an increase in a number of housing subsidies. Some consequences of these decisions are discussed. The chapter concludes with a comparison of alternative reforms of the tax treatment of owner–occupied housing or land.

Housing markets and demand management

The macroeconomic background of rapid expansion in consumer credit, consumer expenditure and imports of consumer goods was summarised in the introduction. In a speech on 15 September, 1986, on 'structural change in housing finance', the Governor of the Bank of England said: 'Some mortgage lending in the UK could give rise to inflationary pressures by accommodating house price increases. Moreover, the leakage of lending secured on a first mortgage, but used for other purposes, may well play a significant role in fuelling the expansion of consumer spending'. He also noted that 'monetary growth is being driven to a considerable extent by the strength of lending to the personal sector in general, and by mortgage lending in particular' (see *Bank of England Quarterly Bulletin*, December 1986).

The Bank of England has been concerned for some time over the problem of equity withdrawal from the housing market as a source of hard-to-control credit expansion (see articles by Davis and Saville, September 1982, and by Drayson, March 1985, in *Bank of England Quarterly Bulletin*). The following summarises the relevant portions of this research. The main ways in which equity withdrawal, which entails generating spendable cash by adding to indebtedness, can occur are the following:

(i) unmortgaged or little mortgaged privately owned dwellings can be sold to persons buying with a mortgage;

(ii) cash deposits by first-time buyers may fall relative to the funds advanced;

(iii) the houses of deceased individuals can be sold to those buying with mortgage. This appears to be a major factor in explaining long-term trends in equity withdrawal as higher and higher proportions of those dying are owner occupiers, usually with little or no mortgage debt;

(iv) owner occupiers may increase debt on existing houses. Some of this has been for real expenditure on home improvements in which case it is not equity withdrawal. But some has probably leaked into other uses;

(v) owner occupiers moving house may increase their mortgages by more than the change in the value of the housing, or they may trade down to a cheaper house.

There are a couple of other factors. For example, the trend towards endowment mortgages away from repayment mortgages tends to reduce capital repayments. On the other hand, falls in mortgage interest rates in the early 1980s have tended to increase capital repayments and so reduce equity withdrawal.

The Bank of England's figures of net equity withdrawal[5] deflated by aggregate personal disposable income for 1965–87 are shown in chart 4.1. There is a clear jump in the series after 1980 when mortgage rationing effectively came to an end. The average United Kingdom house price deflated by per capita personal disposable income is also shown in chart 4.1. Net equity withdrawal is clearly positively correlated with it. However, it is also apparent that the forces, such as restricted mortgage lending and rising interest rates that brought the house price booms of the early and late 1970s under control, acted even earlier on net equity withdrawal. Note the drop in net equity withdrawal in 1973–4 and 1980. The visual impression given by chart 4.1 is that a new equilibrium in relation to house prices was reached in 1982. It remains to be seen whether the further relaxation in rules on lending beginning in 1987 will shift the relationship up further.

An important element in explaining equity withdrawal must be the cost of mortgage capital. Even without tax relief, borrowing on a mortgage is usually the cheapest form of credit. As noted in the 1985 *Quarterly Bulletin* article: 'when, in 1969, personal income tax relief on

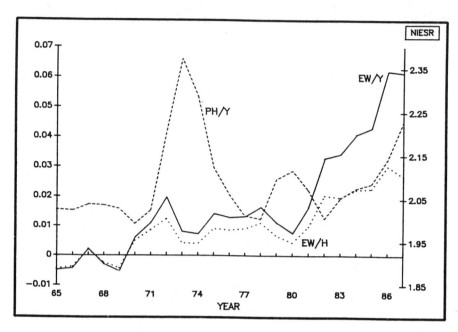

Chart 4.1 Ratio of net equity withdrawal to personal disposable income (EW/Y) and to the owner–occupied housing stock (EW/H) and ratio of house prices to disposable income per capita (P/Y)
(P/Y In logarithms, right – hand scale)

interest payments was first confined to loans for the purpose of house purchase or improvement, a sharply increased trend towards net cash withdrawal from the housing market appeared almost immediately'.

The funds that are released can be spent on other things whether consumer goods or other financial assets. Increased competition by providers of mortgages has driven up the size of loans relative to the earnings capacity of borrowers and, as long as house prices are expected to continue to rise, it is likely that terms will remain generous and the credit expansion will continue. In the last five to six years, the real asset values of the household sector have increased sharply with the boom in equity prices and in house prices. With real wages and dividend income growing strongly too, a strong growth in consumer expenditure was only to be expected. Leakage of equity withdrawal from housing into consumer expenditure is quite analogous to realising capital gains on stocks and shares and spending the proceeds.

The fact that the growth in consumer expenditure can be explained well by these developments does not diminish concern about the skewed nature of the recent demand expansion and its implications for the balance of payments and hence for the exchange rate, interest rates and inflation.

The arguments so far seem as valid now as they did two years ago, though rather more widely acknowledged now, as for example by the Chancellor in his Autumn 1988 Mansion House speech. The earliest warnings of the implications of equity withdrawal were given by Congdon in June 1982, who later forecast that asset price inflation would have substantial effects on consumer expenditure. This is not exactly a new insight given that life–cycle models of the consumption function whichpredict this have been around over thirty years (see Modigliani and Brumberg, 1952). Curiously, as recently as 1988, none of the major macroeconometric models had incorporated housing wealth in any wealth effects that were included in their consumer expenditure equations.

Muellbauer and Murphy (1989) have formalised these effects in an econometric model estimated on annual data for 1956–87. This model pays careful attention to dynamic properties of behaviour through an error correction formulation (see Davidson, Hendry, Srba and Yeo, 1978) and incorporates wealth effects as well as income effects, the relative prices of durables and non–durables, interest rate effects and the shift in behaviour in the 1980s as the incidence of credit constraints on consumer expenditure plainly lessened. This shift has increased somewhat the importance of wealth relative to income. Between end–1982 and end–1987 the net wealth/annual income ratio rose from 3.5 to 4.8 and to around 5 at the end of 1988. Net wealth includes liquid and illiquid financial assets and physical assets but excludes the value of consumer durables and the imputed value of tenancy rights. Our estimates suggest that, other things being equal, an increase from 3.5 to 5 in the net wealth–income ratio would, *in the long run*, raise the ratio of non–durable consumption to income by close to 10 percentage points. Given analogous effects for durable goods, the steady–state savings ratio deteriorates by an even greater amount. In making this comparison, we hold constant the growth rate of real personal disposable income per head, the relative price of non–durables and durables and the ratio of net interest payments to income. Increases in this last ratio cut consumer expenditure, and indeed the increases in short–term interest rates in 1988, reflected with a lag in mortgage interest payments, have been used as a crisis response to the sharp deterioration in the savings ratio and the trade balance experienced in 1988. Our model suggests that, given the size of personal sector debt relative to its holdings of interest–bearing liquid assets in the late 1980s, increases in interest rates have a substantial dampening effect on consumer expenditure.[6] This supports claims made in 1988 by the Chancellor that higher interest rates would bring the overshoot of nominal expenditure in the United Kingdom under control. We return to a discussion of policy issues in the fourth section below.

Housing markets and the supply side
The hypothesis that the United Kingdom housing market affects labour

mobility and so the supply side of the economy is certainly not new (see, for example, Johnson, Salt and Wood, 1974, and reviews of the literature in Minford, Ashton and Peel, 1987). Hughes and McCormick (1981) have studied the effects of the system of allocating council houses on regional mobility and there have been conscious attempts to improve it. At September 1988, 25.2 per cent of dwellings in Great Britain were estimated to be council houses with another 2.5 per cent rented from housing associations. 7.2 per cent were estimated to be privately rented accommodation of which some fraction of occupants pay 'fair' rents; they would generally pay higher rents if they were to move, and one would expect this fact to reduce their mobility. 65.1 per cent of dwellings were estimated to be owner occupied.[7] Some of these are recently purchased council houses previously rented by their owners and there are usually restrictions on resale within a certain number of years which tends to reduce mobility.

The research reported in Bover, Muellbauer and Murphy (1989) examines the effects of housing markets on wage determination and on the aggregate trade–off between unemployment and vacancies in the United Kingdom. Both should be affected by restrictions stemming from housing markets on mobility or on equilibrating migration flows. We argue that regional differences in house prices relative to earnings can give rise to such restrictions, though they may well influence wages and the unemployment/vacancies trade–off in other ways. The cross–section evidence on how migration rates vary with housing tenure categories was incorporated into a mobility index which also included effects from the 1965 and 1974 Rent Acts. This mobility index has a significant effect on the real wage and on unfilled vacancies, given unemployment. House price effects have been split into an average United Kingdom house price/wage effect and the effect of the difference in the house price/earnings ratio between the south–east and the United Kingdom average (chart 4.2).[8] We estimate that the real wage increase from 1984–8 attributable to these two variables was 4.4 percentage points. Back–of–the–envelope calculations suggest that the 1988 acceleration in earnings is consistent with the model. Given the lags and the peak towards the end of 1988 in the regional difference of the house/price earnings ratio, real wage pressure from this source will not diminish in 1989 and will spill over into 1990 at least.

As far as the underlying interpretation is concerned, we were careful to point out that, *in the long run*, relatively high house prices, land prices and wages in the south–east benefit the unemployed elsewhere in Britain. In 1988 evidence has accumulated of new jobs being created outside the south–east and even of jobs being shifted out of the south–east. However, in the short run, strong inflationary pressures for the whole economy can arise from the housing market. This is generated from portfolio demand for housing stimulated by the uniquely tax advantaged status of owner–occupied housing among major asset types. In economic upswings, especially those in which financial liquidity is a factor, as in the early 1970s and in the 1980s, the house price/earnings

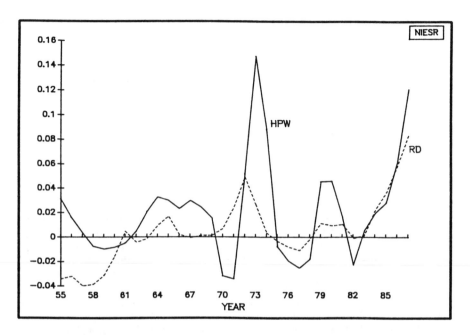

Chart 4.2 House price to wage ratio (HPW) and south–east house price to earnings ratio relative to the UK average (RD)
(in logarithms and weighted by owner – occupancy proportion)

ratio in the south–east rises relatively because housing land is less elastically supplied there. This leads to a 'mobility trap'. As the relative appreciation of house price takes place, households in the south–east are initially more reluctant to move to other areas: they would miss out on the further relative appreciation and may therefore be unable to move back to the south–east at a later date. Thus, few housing slots are freed for potential migrants to the south–east, tending to increase still further the relative appreciation. Households outside the south–east become increasingly unable to bridge the gap in house prices and so are less inclined to migrate.

As the house price/earnings differential approaches a peak, outward migration from the south–east increases. At the same time, the credit constraint for potential migrants to the south–east reaches a maximum. Also by this time additional new housing in the south–east will have been built. This situation cannot persist and speculative expectations are reversed: the result is a rapid fall, as in 1973–5, of the south–east's premium in the house price/earnings differential. The rapidity of the fall is likely to be influenced by the initial reluctance of households outside the south-east to invest in an expensive asset with a lower or negative prospective rate of return compared with their present housing. The peak and early part of this post-peak phase is likely to be a particularly uncomfortable one for firms in the south-east trying to hold on to or to hire workers and, unless labour demand in the south-east is slackening, is likely to be associated with strong wage pressure there. 1973, for example, saw the largest recorded net outflow of people from the south-east, with further large outflows in 1974 and 1975.

This process eventually leads firms and workers to locate outside the south-east and so relieves unemployment in other regions. In the short run, however, this process can impose significant costs. Wage increases in the south-east, quickly followed by even larger price increases there, can give workers in the south-east an incentive to leave and, given credit rationing, be relatively ineffective in attracting new workers. Firms may therefore have to bear the brunt of the resource reallocation shifts engendered by this interaction of housing and labour markets.

McCormick (1989) cites data from the Labour Force Survey for 1982–6 which shows an interesting manual/non-manual dimension in these trends. There has been a rising volume of manual outmigration from the south-east dominating manual inflows. It is plausible that this crowding-out of manual workers has arisen not only from portfolio demand for houses but from demand derived from the growth of employment in financial services whose share of employment is substantially higher in the south-east: in this sector, subsidised mortgages, which are not fully taxed, are prevalent and give staff an incentive to invest heavily in housing.

These fiscal biases in favour of owner-occupation greatly raise the portfolio return to housing relative to that which would prevail in a neutral tax system. Consumer expenditure is influenced by house price increases through wealth effects and the increase in collateral available for borrowing. This tends not only to increase aggregate consumer expenditure and imports but also to increase regional disparities. The greater increase in consumer expenditure in the south-east has regional multiplier effects which feed back through household demand into south-east house prices. This adds to the overshooting tendencies discussed above. These tendencies have been exacerbated by the liberalisation of credit markets in the 1980s and would be reduced by a more neutral tax treatment of owner-occupied housing. Our results emphasise the hazards of liberalising financial markets while enormous fiscal distortions remain in place.

This structural interpretation of house price effects may be contrasted with the most plausible of the non-structural interpretations set out in Bover, Muellbauer and Murphy (1989). This argues that a good proxy for the regional difference in labour demand shocks may be the regional difference in the house price to earnings ratio. A positive labour demand shock in the south-east combined with a negative demand shock elsewhere leaving aggregate labour demand unchanged is very likely to raise aggregate wages: it is plausible that wages respond in greater degree to positive shocks than negative ones and the effect is enhanced by the fact that unemployment in the south–east has been below the United Kingdom average for the last thirty years. However, our work on determinants of the regional differences in the house price/earnings ratio suggests that differential labour demand shocks are only a part of the story.

In recent work, Muellbauer and Murphy (1988a and b) have studied regional and international migration for the United Kingdom. This work lends strong support to a structural interpretation of the house price effects we find in the wage equation and in the unemployment/vacancies equation. The most significant determinant of net migration between the south–east and the rest of the United Kingdom is the two–year moving average of the regional difference in the house price/earnings ratio. Other important influences on these migration flows are regional differences in labour demand growth,[9] in unemployment rates and changes in the age composition of the population. The tenure structure of housing influences net migration in a way which is consistent with survey evidence. Changes in international net migration into the United Kingdom affect regional migration: since international migration is disproportionately to and from the south–east, increased net immigration into the United Kingdom tends to crowd out some of the regional migration to the south–east.

The national house price/earnings ratio is a major influence on international net migration into the United Kingdom. Relative growth and the labour market situation in the United Kingdom compared with other major economies have important effects on net international migration. For example, with the United Kingdom recovering from the 1980–81 recession, 1983–5 saw a sharp pick–up of net inward migration. A rising house price/earnings ratio in the United Kingdom dampened this in 1986–7 and for 1988–9 we predict net outflows.

International migration into the United Kingdom affects the south–east disproportionately so that the net outflow from the south–east outside the United Kingdom is likely to be around 30,000 individuals in 1988. The total net loss of population in the south–east from migration in 1988 could easily be 100,000 individuals.

Such migration flows have economic consequences whose regional dimension was discussed above. Another of them is a brain and skills drain abroad given that two thirds of employed emigrants have in recent years been in the professional and managerial category. This is likely to intensify pressure on pay in the upper echelons of the labour market which are not well represented by the unemployment and vacancies statistics. We suspect that this is part of the reason why the United Kingdom house price/wage ratio shows up as strongly as it does in our wage equation. Another consequence is a drain on the capital account of the balance of payments. In our December 1988 report we suggest that in 1988, the net drain could be as large as £3–5 billion and even larger in 1989 though it is unlikely to show up in the CSO's Pink Book statistics.

None of this work is intended to show that markets do not work. For example, we are well aware of the age structure of internal migration flows: migrants into the south–east tend to be younger than migrants out. The retired out–migrants vacate housing slots which potentially may be occupied by in–migrants who can afford them. Furthermore, as Holmans (1988) and Gordon (Chapter 5) point out, the migration patterns in and out of the south–east which we have studied may have somewhat attenuated implications for labour markets. A substantial part of regional emigration from the south–east is with the adjoining regions: East Anglia, the east midlands and the south–west. It is likely that some of the emigrants continue to work in the same south–east location and are merely trading lower housing costs for longer commuter trips by moving out. Efficient trade–offs betwen commuting costs and housing costs are all part of the functioning of the market system.

Nevertheless, Gordon acknowledges that actual net migration to the south, consisting of the south–east and the adjoining regions, has been much below the migration required by relative labour demand growth. Part of the reason lies in house prices which can increase for extraneous reasons connected not with demands for living space generated in the labour market, but with demands that originate with the tax system (for example, the abolition of domestic rates or variations in housing subsidies), or derive from the portfolio demand for houses given their historically high real rates of return. Such price changes have repercussions for labour markets which, in the short to medium run, can impair the functioning of the supply side of the economy.

The reform of housing market institutions and other policy alternatives

Fundamentally, the problems discussed in the introduction and in the two following sections result to a considerable extent from two basic institutional features of the housing market. The first is the system of planning controls laid down in the Town and Country Planning Acts. There seem to be strong environmental, social and aesthetic arguments in favour of some kind of intervention by public authorities in the operation of private markets for land.[10]

From the point of view of the United Kingdom economy's demand side, the second section above pointed to the high levels of the ratios of houses and land prices as well as in financial wealth to incomes prevailing in 1988 and at the time of writing (chart 4.3). At such levels, the United Kingdom personal savings ratio is unsustainably low and the balance of payments deficit is unsustainably high unless a compensating downward correction occurs in other components of net wealth. However, though financial markets can overshoot, there are good arguments to suggest that the values of United Kingdom financial assets are closer to their fundamental economic values than is true for United Kingdom house and residential land values.[11] One reason is that fiscal distortions are small compared with those for housing and residential land. The other reason is that financial markets are internationally

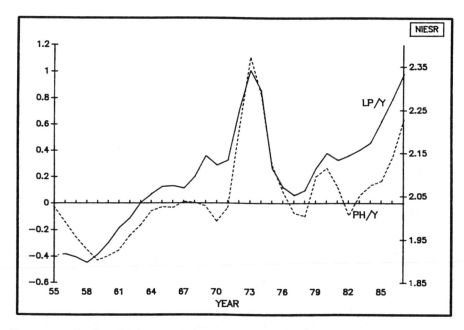

Chart 4.3 Ratio of house prices (PH/Y, *right – hand scale*) and land prices (LP/Y) to disposable income per capita
(*in logarithms*)

competitive and there are no major restrictions on the mobility of finance. In contrast, nothing in the United Kingdom can be less mobile than land though the mobility of population and other factors of production can be a partial substitute. *Ultimately*, as we suggested in our discussion of international migration (Muellbauer and Murphy, 1988b), such migration helps to prevent housing and land values relative to income in the United Kingdom getting too far out of line with those in other countries. The balance of payments itself will *ultimately* lead to a correction of the United Kingdom's net wealth to income ratio. But both processes are likely to be experienced as rather unpleasant and involve real damage to the long–run productive potential of the economy.

The 1988–9 policy response to excessive domestic demand has been to raise short–term interest rates. As our recent research on consumer expenditure establishes, there are direct effects from interest rates on consumer expenditure as well as indirect effects which operate via net wealth. The direct effects arise from the asymmetric behaviour of borrowers and lenders when interest rates increase. Borrowers in floating rate markets, which United Kingdom mortgage and personal loan markets primarily are, are forced by liquidity constraints resulting from higher rates to cut their expenditure. Their cut is greater than the increase by borrowers who find their investment income higher than expected, especially when, as in 1988–9, aggregate interest payments on debt significantly exceed aggregate interest receipts on liquid assets. However, we also find that a given increase in the ratio of net interest payments to income now has a smaller effect on consumer expenditure than was true before credit constraints were relaxed beginning in 1981–2. Under current credit conditions, lenders are likely to take a favourable view towards creditors rolling part of the higher interest charges into increased debt and a variety of special incentive schemes have emerged to help first–time house buyers and others.

There are other difficulties in making high short–term interest rates stick. In effect, most mortgage borrowers can convert a United Kingdom mortgage into a German or Swiss mortgage in a transaction taking only a few minutes in a High Street bank. In the forward currency market which, in German marks, is liquid up to five years ahead, the difference between a forward rate and the spot rate equals the international interest rate differential. Thus someone with a £30,000 United Kingdom mortgage who wishes to pay effectively the German interest rate for six months can buy a £30,000 contract to buy sterling in six months time. At the end of the period he or she collects the interest rate differential minus any currency depreciation which has taken place. The latter can plausibly be expected to be small or even turn into an appreciation given the anti–inflationary United Kingdom policy stance and the attractions of high short–term rates in the United Kingdom for international short–term funds. Any gains are treated as capital gains by the United Kingdom tax authorities and, for most owner occupiers, are likely to come under the exemption limit, thus being tax free. At the same time, full tax relief on mortgage interest payments at high United Kingdom interest rates is received on the continuing £30,000 mortgage. As home owners and other borrowers at short rates become wise to these possibilities, sterling is likely to appreciate to a level where the currency risk of such schemes begins to appear unacceptable to most borrowers.

Another difficulty making high short–term rates stick arises from the 'inverted yield curve', that is, from the fact that long–term rates in the United Kingdom are much below short–term rates.[12] Sooner or later, it seems inevitable that financial innovation will lead to the introduction of effectively fixed–rate mortgages at interest rates close to current long–term rates. The flowering of fixed–rate schemes of, admittedly, limited duration at the time of writing is an early sign of such trends.

As far as house prices are concerned, all researchers are agreed that higher short–term interest rates dampen the demand for house purchase and so house price increases. But by the above arguments, one might well expect a diminishing effectiveness from such a policy at a national level. By dampening the demand for house purchase in general, the tendency is for regional differences in house prices to fall. In the circumstances of 1988–9, where south–east house and land prices are at record levels relative to those outside the south–east (chart 4.2), both prospective relative capital gains and the high differential give individuals and firms an incentive to relocate outside the highest price areas. This and the wealth effects on expenditure now being experienced more strongly outside the south–east should give a substantial boost to employment growth feeding back on house prices outside the south–east. The effects on the housing component of national net wealth of rising house prices outside the south–east and static or gently declining house prices in the south–east may be merely to stabilise the net wealth to income ratio at a level that promises continuing excess demand pressure.

Another concern about high levels of short–term interest rates as the sole policy response must be that the currency appreciation which is entailed may make it even harder to correct the external balance and can do long–term damage to the development of the United Kingdom's productive potential. The indiscriminate nature of interest rate increases, for example, the problems they pose for small companies (see Wadhwani, 1986) and their effect on the retail price index and so on wages via cost of living contracts are other difficulties.

The United Kingdom's problem of excessive consumer demand is not merely a cyclical one but a structural one requiring structural reforms. Such a structural reform should, in due course (a) bring down national ratios of housing and land prices to incomes. This would lower the net wealth to income ratio and so consumer expenditure below what they would otherwise have been. From the point of view of the supply side of the United Kingdom economy, in particular of a less inflationary, better functioning labour market, a reform of housing market institutions should result in (b) a better regional economic balance; (c) a more efficient utilisation of the stock of dwellings especially in areas of high labour demand; (d) a reduction in the tendency of house prices to overshoot speculatively; (e) closely linked to (c) and (d), the removal of the current bias in tax incentives against supplying rented accommodation, and a general increase in the supply elasticities of housing; (f) the removal of tax distortions affecting important saving, investment and labour supply decisions; (g) the resulting administrative and tax collection costs not being excessive.

Bearing these criteria in mind, let us examine recent government legislation in the housing area. First, consider the abolition of domestic rates in Scotland in 1989 and in England and Wales in 1990 and their replacement by a Community Charge or Poll Tax. This was the subject of Muellbauer (1987). This argued that domestic rates were an unsatisfactory tax for two main reasons. Firstly, rates are based on relatively arbitrary and outdated valuations. Secondly, the 'poundage' charged by different local authorities often tends to be high in areas where the needs of the local population are high and property values low. Thus, they offer a perverse incentive for the location of business and people which perpetuates the problems of relatively depressed areas. Two other objections put forward by the government, that domestic rates are insufficiently a service charge and that too many residents who can vote in local elections do not pay rates are much less convincing.

In terms of the United Kingdom's aggregate demand problems, the proposed rates abolition unambiguously raises the demand for housing and so increases house prices in the short to medium term. Hughes (1988) predicts a real increase of United Kingdom house prices of around 18 per cent while Spencer (1988) argues for a somewhat higher figure and accepts the argument that the increase is likely to be somewhat greater in the south-east where the supply elasticity of land is lower. This increases the risk of economic problems associated with aggregate demand too heavily biased towards consumption. In terms of the aggregate supply objectives outlined above, it is very likely that the proposed reform of domestic rates would be perverse.

As far as (b), achieving a more efficient utilisation of the existing stock of dwellings is concerned, existing domestic rates are less than ideal because of the outdated and sometimes arbitrary rateable values and because of the regionally regressive variations in the poundage. However, removing residential property from the tax net altogether is worse still.

As far as (d), reducing the tendency for house prices to overshoot speculatively, is concerned, the existing system of domestic rates is defective because revaluations are so infrequent and because rates do not vary sufficiently with property values across different localities. Nevertheless, the prospect of a possible property revaluation in future may dampen the variability of house prices. The removal of a residential property tax altogether takes away even this dampener and by eliminating the holding cost of leaving a property empty makes it more attractive to engage in speculative hoarding of property.

As far as (e), improving the elasticity of supply of housing, is concerned, speculative hoarding can temporarily make supply elasticities of housing perverse. Thus, a wage increase signalling a local increase in labour demand can, at times, result in a disproportionate increase in house prices which temporarily may even reduce the local supply of available housing. But increasing the supply of rented accommodation is probably the best hope for increasing the responsiveness of housing to labour market needs. Under the present system there is some discrimination in the tax system against owners of privately rented accommodation since they are liable for capital gains tax while owner-occupiers are not. Domestic rates as a tax on imputed rents can be seen as a very rough equivalent for owner occupiers of income tax on rents received by landlords. Their abolition increases the fiscal discrimination against landlords relative to owner occupiers. However, in the last year this has been offset by the granting of large tax subsidies via the Business Expansion Scheme to investment in rented accommodation. One of the main obstacles to rent decontrol is the high level of free market rents. Since this level is directly related to the level of land and house prices, anything such as the abolition of domestic rates which raises land and house prices further makes rent decontrol and so the re–emergence of a private rented sector harder to achieve.

Let us now turn to criterion (f), the removal of tax distortions affecting saving, investment and work decisions. Two defects of the present system can be pointed out. One, noted by Johnson,[13] which current proposals leave unaltered, is that, with corporation tax down to 25 per cent for small companies, the interest subsidy to high marginal rate taxpayers of mortgage interest relief discriminates against putting money into a business as opposed to a house. This would seem to contradict the government's desire to stimulate the growth of small businesses. The other is the poverty trap created by rate rebates. This can only become worse under the new system since the community charge bears so heavily on low income, working people. The 80 per cent rebate together with the benefit increase to those receiving supplementary and unemployment benefit creates an incentive to withdraw from the labour force and claim benefits. For a government so strongly committed to sharpening economic incentives this is a most unfortunate by–product of the proposed reforms.

Finally on (g), tax collection costs, it is worth noting how expensive it will be to collect the community charge. This is not only because so many more individuals have to be approached than under rates, but because of the difficulty and expense of catching those who try to evade the tax. In this connection, the fear must not be discounted that a new stratum of drifters and vagrants trying to escape the community charge will be brought into being, and that crime and disrespect for the law will increase as a result.

Apart from the abolition of domestic rates, three other aspects of government policies on housing need discussion. One concerns the major cutbacks in council house building. Whatever one may say about the deficiencies of the system of allocating council houses, the cuts in building in the south–east have surely constrained the available manual labour supply there. Recently, more public funds have become available for the provision of subsidised housing through housing associations while public sector tenants are being given the right to choose a new landlord, typically some kind of housing association. The second concerns the 1988 Housing Act, whose provision on private renting came into force on 15 January, 1989. Under the Act virtually all new lettings become new–form assured tenancies for one year at a time or short–hold tenancies for six months at a time. Such tenancies allow a market rent to be agreed between landlord and tenant and for the agreement to include regular rent revisions. Security of tenure can be overridden if the landlord wishes to redevelop or sell the property. Existing fair–rent tenancies can continue but can be expected gradually to evaporate as tenants move, die or are offered incentives (and sometimes indeed harassment) to quit. The third aspect is the envisaged expansion of housing benefit to cope with the stresses of higher rents both in the private sector and in the public sector where the government is pressing local authorities to reduce subsidies.

These are policies that could all be welcomed in an environment where prices of building land and so of free market rents were substantially lower in relation to incomes than is now the case. Between 1981 and the second quarter of 1988 the price of an average building plot divided by per capita personal disposable income in the United Kingdom went from 1.6 to 4.1 in England and Wales, from 2.3 to 7.2 in Greater London and from 2.2 to 7.4 in the rest of the south–east.[14] Though house prices and free market rents have not increased relative to incomes at quite these staggering rates, it is obvious enough that, in much of the country, tenants on average manual earnings cannot afford reasonable accommodation at free market rents. To put it another way, landlords cannot earn an economic return on their investment at rents which such tenants could afford (see Chapter 7 for further discussion of this issue).

So far, it seems that the government response to these problems is to pile on more subsidies. The Business Expansion Scheme subsidies for investment in rented accommodation reduce the tax bias against the rented sector in comparison with owner occupation. But a fundamental objection against both it and expanded housing benefit subsidies is that they drive up or at least support land prices. In other words, much of the subsidy accrues to landowners rather than lower income tenants. Housing benefit has another very major defect. This is the so–called 'taper', that is, the rate at which housing benefit is withdrawn as tenants' incomes rise. It seems virtually certain that the effective marginal tax rate faced by such tenants will be at least 65 per cent and could be over 100 per cent when withdrawal of community charge rebates, income tax and national insurance contributions are taken into account. The government thus faces a very serious policy dilemma. On the one hand it could allow a sharp deterioration in the living standard of low income workers to occur by limiting housing benefit, and this on top of the dramatic widening of economic inequality that has occurred in the 1980s (see *Economic Trends*, December 1988). On the other, it could allow a sharp deterioration in the work incentives and hence the labour supply of low income workers. This is both inflationary and damaging to the functioning of the economy.

So far, the government has shied away from the reform of the tax treatment of housing which is evidently required. However, the 1988 budget restricted mortgage interest tax relief to one per property as opposed to one per individual[15] and eliminated tax relief on loans for home improvements. There are basically four policy options. The first is the abolition of mortgage interest tax relief or perhaps its restriction to a once–only limited period of, say, five years. Apart from the Prime Minister's pledge to retain mortgage interest tax relief, a major objection is that this policy alone is likely to bear most heavily, at least in the first instance, on first–time buyers. Given imperfect credit markets, the life–cycle phase at which first–time buyers typically find themselves is one where they face more severe credit constraints than later on. Also, there is a general efficiency argument that suggests that households should face similar after–tax interest rates on borrowing and lending. These arguments favour keeping the Prime Minister's pledge.

A second alternative is a housing transaction tax similar to sharply raising stamp duty. This would do so much obvious damage to mobility that it is not worth considering further in the presence of better alternatives.

A third alternative is to extend capital gains tax (CGT) to main residences. King (1988) has proposed a version of CGT with rollover relief. Thus, someone selling a house would only pay CGT on a gain which was not reinvested in another house. Such rollover relief is obviously required to prevent the damaging effects on mobility which otherwise would be similar to those of a transactions tax. While this is a good idea in principle, the worry must be that CGT is too full of escape routes. Unless these are sharply restricted, a consequence might therefore be to discourage individuals from cashing in until their CGT position is most favourable, for example, at death or when other losses can be offset. This might therefore reduce the flow of properties coming onto the market, paradoxically reducing occupancy rates and supporting land and house prices.

As suggested earlier, there are arguments in favour of a fourth alternative, a tax on the market value of houses. This would be integrated into the national income tax system by the Inland Revenue. Market values would be based on historical market prices indexed annually to local house price indices which the Inland Revenue could compute as a byproduct of its collection of stamp duty on close to one million house sales per year. 3 per cent of the market value above some exemption limit envisaged as being added to each tax unit's taxable income with appropriate reductions in the overall tax rate or increases in allowances to keep overall tax revenue to what it would otherwise have been.

In a *Sunday Times* article,[16] it was suggested that a sensible alternative to taxing houses was to tax only the underlying residential land value. This has two advantages. The first is that the incentive against carrying out improvements which stems from taxing the market value of houses is removed.[17] The second is that vacant land zoned for residential development would be taxed too. This would soon increase the supply of such land for housing, and for a given amount of tax revenue collected, would have much larger consequences on land prices and so on house prices than a tax on house values *per se*. To put it another way, a given reduction in the ratio of land and house prices to income could be achieved by collecting a substantially smaller amount of revenue from owner occupiers. This would therefore be politically more acceptable.

The main objection against taxing residential land values is the valuation problem. The market in vacant building plots in old established residential areas is much thinner than the market for houses in such areas. In the United States, where property taxes are a major source of state and local revenue, there is sophisticated valuation industry using regression analysis to make valuations. There is little difficulty in using such techniques to impute land values given house price data and housing characteristics. The imputations need to be cross–checked against the available information on the contemporary costs of constructing a dwelling with given characteristics and against those transactions in vacant plots which take place. In the United Kingdom the administrative structure already exists. District valuers remain in being since they will have to produce valuations on which the uniform business rate will be based. It seems plausible that they would find estimating current residential land values rather easier than imputing the 1973 rent that a present day residential property might have attracted. Any problems would be eased further by computer access to the data files held by the Inland Revenue valuation office.

Whether the imputation to be included in the Inland Revenue's definition of taxable income is based on the value of residences or on the value of the underlying land, it must be acknowledged that there are administrative costs in achieving integration with the income tax system. The Inland Revenue tax offices are not organised primarily on the basis of where taxpayers live but on where they work. Many taxpayers never submit tax returns given the PAYE system. The alternative to integration is to apply the standard income tax rate of 25 per cent to, say, 4 per cent of the market value of the residential land over and above some exemption limit and associate a tax liability with each piece of property rather than with particular income taxpayers. One could then extend the existing system of domestic rates rebates to ensure that those with low cash incomes were given tax rebates.

The progressivity of the system varies with the exemption limit. In current circumstances this might be set at perhaps £15,000 per plot so that 1 per cent per annum of the plot value over and above £15,000 would be paid in tax. This would ensure that many owner occupiers escaped the tax altogether. Landlords would be able to deduct all or part of the tax from tax due on their rent receipts.

This reform proposal satisfies all the criteria set out earlier in this section. It would lower land and house prices relative to income, thus bringing the personal sector's net wealth into a more sustainable relationship with income. This would help raise the personal sector savings ratio. It would contribute to a better regional economic balance for reasons similar to those that justify the government's new uniform business rate. It would lead to a more efficient utilisation of land and buildings especially in areas of pressure. It would reduce the tendency of land and house prices to overshoot speculatively by increasing the discounted value of the prospective tax burden when these prices increase. It would remove a major part of the current tax bias against supplying rented accommodation and would increase the supply elasticity of land and hence of housing. It would reduce the tax advantages to small entrepreneurs of investing in housing and land instead of ploughing profits back into the business. At lower land prices and, eventually, lower free market rents relative to income, the unemployment trap arising from housing benefit would be reduced. The administrative costs do not look excessive since existing administrative structures are retained.

There are some other advantages that stem from taxing the market value of residential land. One is that a better tax base is hard to imagine. Residential land has a low elasticity of supply and the price elasticity of demand is probably also low. Taxing it therefore creates few distortions. It is a tax which is relatively easy to collect: land is hard to move or disguise! As a 'betterment tax' it is an excellent way of taxing beneficiaries of public investment projects, many of whose benefits accrue in increases in the value of advantageously located land. Another advantage concerns the automatic stabilisation that can be expected from it. Periods in which land prices have increased fastest have tended to be periods of inflationary pressure. The inclusion of land values as part of the tax base increases the automatic response of the tax take to such inflationary pressure and conversely in periods of deflation. This makes it possible for the authorities to operate less interventionist policies.

In our research we have tried to make precise the mechanisms by which house and land prices can affect decisions on expenditure, migration, labour supply, location of economic activities, wage negotiations and hence various other economic outcomes. We have also tried to understand house and land prices as themselves the outcomes of economic forces. But there may still be something we have not succeeded in pinning down precisely. Under the institutional arrangements that have prevailed for the 25 years, there is a subtly corrupting bias in favour of inflation which has operated for decision makers who are owner occupiers at all levels, whether employers, trade unionists, civil servants or politicians. This results from the palpable personal benefits from, or at least insurance against, inflation which their status as owner occupiers has provided. A tax based on land prices themselves substantially reduces these benefits of insurance. At the margin, it should therefore result in the choice of policies with lower inflationary risk and, probably therefore, policies that favour a generally less uncertain economic environment. In the past, the perpetual tendency of growth in the United Kingdom to stimulate inflation, has surely been a major barrier to the achievement of steady growth.

Appendix: An overshooting model of house prices and wages
In the appendix to Chapter 2, Ermisch sets out a little general equilibrium model of wage and house price determination in the long run. What is particularly attractive about his model is the simple way in which the regional discussion is handled. However, his neglect of dynamic issues makes his model incapable of illuminating the short–term interactions of labour and housing markets with which the third section above was concerned. In the following, some dynamic effects in the context of the stylised rational expectations model of house price overshooting are introduced.

Notation: L^d = labour demand, L^s = labour supply, w = log real wage,

Housing and the National Economy

p = log real house price, H = housing stock, x = other influences on the real wage, for example, union power. All variables refer to a particular region, say the south–east, with the rest of the economy being taken as given, following Ermisch.

The behavioural equations are as follows:

Labour demand
$$L^d = c_0 - c_1 w + c_2 p + c_3 \dot{p} \tag{A1}$$

where the cs are positive parameters. Labour demand falls as the wage increases but, because of derived labour demand from wealth effects on consumption, increases with the price and with capital gains in housing $\dot{p}$. [18]

Labour supply
$$L^s = b_0 + b_1 w - b_2 p + b_3 \dot{p} \tag{A2}$$

where the bs are positive parameters. Labour supply increases with the wage but is lower at a higher real house price. On the other hand, anticipated capital gains can induce migration so that b_3 is positive.

Housing demand
$$H = \beta_0 + L^s + \beta_1 w - \beta_2 p + \beta_3 \dot{p} = \beta'_0 + \beta'_1 w - \beta'_2 p + \beta'_3 \dot{p} \tag{A3}$$

where the βs are positive parameters. Housing demand increases with labour supply, the wage and anticipated gains in house prices but decreases with the level of house prices.

Stock adjustment supply equation of housing
The rate of change of the stock of housing $\dot{H}$ is given by

$$\dot{H} = \delta_0 - \delta_1 w + \delta_2 p - \delta_3 H - \delta_4 \dot{p} \tag{A4}$$

where the δs are positive parameters. The negative response of the supply flow of houses to wages is via the cost of building workers. δ_3 measures the deterioration rate of houses: every period a proportion of the stock wears out. The negative response to anticipated capital gains in house prices (or indeed land prices) represents speculative hoarding: if prices are expected to be higher in future, it pays to postpone sales. To the level of the house price, supply, of course, responds positively.

Wage equation
$$w = G(L^d - L^s) + g_1 p + g_2 x \tag{A5}$$

The real wage responds positively but in a non–linear fashion (G">0) to excess demand for labour and positively to house prices and other factors x such as union power. The positive response to house prices, or more properly land prices, which is in addition to the role played by house

68

prices in determining $L^d - L^s$, can be interpreted as a cost of living effect. This arises because land prices are reflected in measures of the cost of living but not as part of the cost of producing value added. Economic theory and our research also suggest a non-linear effect on wages from the rate of change of excess demand for labour but this is omitted here for the sake of simplicity.

To analyse the dynamics of the system of equations (A1–A5) it is helpful to begin by isolating the effect of wages. Holding w constant, only housing demand (A3) and housing supply (A4) remain relevant and give a fairly conventional rational expectations model of the housing market. In this p is a 'jump variable'. A phase diagram in p,H space illustrates the effect of a demand expansion (β_0 increases). From an initial equilibrium at E_1 where the steady state loci $\dot{H} = 0$ (downward sloping) and $\dot{p} = 0$ (upward sloping) intersect, an increase in β_0 shifts both loci upwards giving a new long–run equilibrium at E_2, at which p and H are higher. Under rational expectations with the housing stock given at any moment, the result of the parameter shift is a jump appreciation of the house price at the initial equilibrium H to the new saddle path and then convergence along it to E_2. Thus, the price overshoots and then falls gently to its steady state value.

Let us now consider the equation system in which the real wage is endogenous. From equations (A1) and (A2) we can solve for excess demand for labour $L^d - L^s$ as a function of w, p and $\dot{p}$. Substituting this into the wage equation (A5) gives a solution for w as a function of p, $\dot{p}$ and x with which w can be eliminated from (A3) and (A4). Linearising, the result is a two equation system formally similar to (A3) and (A4) with w held fixed. However, the parameters are now different and x has been introduced as a new argument in the system. Endogenising w is roughly equivalent to reducing β'_2. This is because w is an increasing function of p and β'_1 is positive. This steepens the $\dot{p} = 0$ locus and is likely to steepen the convergent path which increases the extent of the house price overshoot.

This is an oversimplified model with oversimplified dynamics. I do not believe that the behaviour of participants in the United Kingdom housing market is consistent with generally held rational expectations. For example, we have econometric evidence of an extrapolative element in forecasting real returns on housing which suggests that even greater overshooting can occur than under rational expectations. Nevertheless, the model does say something about reality. If one interprets the shift in housing demand β_0 as representing the liberalisation of credit markets after 1981 or the abolition of domestic rates, the model helps explain the house price appreciation that has occurred. It also explains the crowding out of part of the south–east's labour supply and upward pressure on wages both from this and from the direct effect of house or land prices on wages. Had liberalisation of credit and the abolition of domestic rates been accompanied by a tax reform of the type favoured in the fourth section above, the offsetting reduction in demand for houses (and land) could have prevented the house and land price explosion that occurred. It seems plausible that such a reform would also have shifted some of the other structural parameters in a helpful direction. I have in mind here the supply elasticity of housing and the parameters attaching to some of the capital gains terms which contribute to the overshooting phenomenon.

Notes

1   A first draft of this paper was circulated in January 1987 and with small revisions in May 1987. The parts of that paper dealing with the abolition of domestic rates and the introduction of the community charge or poll tax were somewhat expanded and appeared as Muellbauer (1987). The present chapter updates the rest of the original paper in the light of joint research with Olympia Bover, David Hendry and Anthony Murphy and of economic events two years on.

2   The further increase in vacancies since then has, at least, been accompanied by falling unemployment.

3   *Industrial Relations Review and Report* no. 429, 1988.

4   For example, *Financial Times*, 28 November, 1988.

5   The Bank of England's figures are deflated by the number of owner occupied dwellings from *Housing and Construction Statistics*, table 9.3. For a guide to an alternative definition of equity withdrawal see Holmans (1986).

6   Though we have evidence that a given increase in the ratio of net interest payments to income is having a less powerful dampening effect on consumer expenditure than was the case before 1982.

7   These figures come from *Housing and Construction Statistics*, part 2, no. 35, 1988.

8   These variables enter at average lags of respectively three and two years and are weighted by the proportion of owner occupiers. The current values for 1956–87 are plotted in chart 4.2.

9   The two–year rate of growth of employment is the measure we use. Hughes and McCormick (Chapter 6), who have studied a short run of years using the Labour Force Survey, do not control adequately for such an effect. This, together with lack of variation in the data, may help to account for their claim that house price effects on migration are weak.

10   Personally, I take the view that present planning policy gives inadequate protection to urban lungs of open space while

overprotecting agricultural land of no special merit against the construction of new communities. See Evans (1988) for a much more critical view of present planning policy.

11   Behind the increase in *financial* wealth relative to income lie a number of favourable developments: global disinflation, a fall in the prices of goods we import compared with those we produce, the return of rates of economic growth, productivity growth and company profitability to match those of the 'golden age' of the late 1950s to the early 1970s, and high United Kingdom oil revenues which have made government surpluses possible.

12   This in turn is partly the result of public sector financial surpluses which are resulting in the retirement of government stock and a resulting stock shortage in the long–term debt market.

13   In *Lloyds Bank Economic Bulletin*, **73**, January 1985.

14   These calculations apply the Department of the Environment's weighted land price indices to 1981 prices of average building plots. The longer history of land prices, see Holmans (1988) for data, is shown in chart 4.3 where pre–1963 values were obtained from an econometric model linking land prices, house prices and building costs.

15   By giving individuals five months before the new rules came into force, the announcement in March 1988 had the unfortunate short–term effect of driving house prices yet higher.

16   'Tax houses as part of income', *Sunday Times*, 11 September 1988.

17   However, note that this is reduced by measuring market value by historical cost indexed to the local house price index. But that in turn can create some incentives against mobility.

18   More properly, $c_2p + c_3\dot{p}$ should be replaced by $\int_{s=0}^{\infty}\lambda(s)p(s)ds$ where λ is positive for small s to indicate a rapid consumer demand response to housing wealth and λ negative for large s to indicate a longer term negative response of labour demand to higher land prices as firms move out or do not move in.

Comment on Chapter 4

Peter Westaway

Muellbauer has given a very clear account of the work that he and his colleagues have done. The chapter splits into two main sections, the first describing the different ways in which the housing market impinges on both the demand and supply of the economy, the second investigating the policy implications of this.

Given the strong policy recommendations that emerge, it is tempting to focus immediately on the latter. In particular, the interesting discussion of the issue of a replacement for domestic rates includes a very persuasive critique of the case for the poll tax. The topicality of this area has been reflected in the correspondence surrounding Muellbauer's work in the *Financial Times*. However, what I would like to focus on very much reflects my own interest as a member of a macromodelling team, and in that sense, I am following on from the remarks made by Meen in Chapter 3. The key questions seem to be as follows: what are the channels through which house prices affect the macroeconomy; and what are the implications for macromodellers?

As far as these questions are concerned, this chapter looks at two key areas – on the supply side focussing on earnings behaviour and on the demand side looking at consumption. But before discussing each of these areas one should urge caution to anyone attempting to do empirical work on house prices. Two dangers in particular may be highlighted. First, it is crucial to acknowledge that, although house prices may have some role to play in the determination of consumers' behaviour, they are also likely to have many of the same causes. As a consequence, this problem of simultaneity needs careful treatment if the two different roles of house prices as both symptom and cause are not to be confused. Second, there is a tendency for modellers to clutch at any new phenomenon which sounds plausible whenever existing models have broken down. In fact this remark probably applies less to Muellbauer than to city commentators and, if the Autumn Statement is anything to go by, to the Chancellor.

Much has already been said about the earnings equation developed by Muellbauer. At the risk of covering old ground, a few queries about the precise role of house prices in the equation are pertinent. It is useful to consider the role of house prices in the context of a stylised earnings relationship. This may be seen to comprise four main effects; cyclical effects reflecting the strength of demand; employer/employee wedge effects reflecting the different costs and benefits facing employers and employees for a given level of earnings; mismatch effects, for example, picking up impediments to labour mobility; and structural effects, such as trade union influences. In which of these categories do house price effects, as postulated by Muellbauer, fall?

On the one hand, the aggregate house price to earnings ratio is interpreted here as a wedge effect. On the other, the regional house price dispersion measure, which is assumed to impinge on migration decisions, may be interpreted as a mismatch effect. Importantly, in both cases, house prices affect earnings via their effect on the cost of living. Given this channel of influence, is the effect specified correctly? A number of doubts arise with Muellbauer's specification. First, if the term is attempting to pick up housing costs, why is no account taken of the most important component of the cost of housing services, that is, the mortgage payment. Second, if regional price levels differ, this will also affect the relative cost of living. Third, and importantly, other elements of the user cost such as the expected capital gain on housing, is excluded from the empirical work, and this omission seems strange since the likely importance of this effect is mentioned in the text of the chapter.

Another criticism often made of the role of house prices in earnings equations is that they are merely picking up cyclical effects. This view seems to be supported by Meen (Chapter 3) who shows that the inclusion of an unemployment term renders house prices insignificant. Recent work at the National Institute has also emphasised that cyclical effects need to be treated carefully. By looking at the problem in a cointegrating framework, it is suggested that there may be separate cyclical effects from unemployment and productivity. The implication of this for Muellbauer's methodology is that the precise method used to de–trend productivity may have an important influence on the significance of other cyclical variables, including house prices.

Turning now to consumer spending, the other main area where Muellbauer claims house prices to be important, there has been a tendency for economic commentators to make statements far stronger than the evidence warrants. Of course, it is clear from the theory that there are a number of channels through which house prices might affect consumer spending. However, what is less clear, as is claimed by Muellbauer, is that these effects can be found easily in an econometric sense.

Rightly, much is made of the influence of mortgage equity withdrawal. It is well known since the work of Holmans that this may arise from different sources. However, what is less often emphasised is that the different types will have very different implications for consumer spending. On the one hand, 'structural' equity withdrawal, caused, for example, by inheritance of properties, may have a limited tendency to leak into consumer spending; on the other, those mortgages that are deliberately taken out for the purposes of consumer spending will be more akin to ordinary consumer credit and will thus have a direct and strong effect on consumption. To further complicate matters, the proportions attributable to these different types of equity withdrawal have been changing, and for the most recent data, are unknown.

On introducing housing wealth into consumption equations, it is certainly true that there may be a direct effect from house prices if people are encouraged to trade down when the value of their assets rises. However, the mere insertion of a net housing wealth term in the consumption equation is much too simplistic and raises a number of questions.   If this is capturing a creditworthiness effect, the appropriate treatment of credit rationing must be ensured and is anyway part of the more general problem of how consumer borrowing is determined; indeed, as Ermisch notes in Chapter 2, this argument implies that house price effects would only be switched in when rationing ends. If it is picking up a standard wealth effect, how do we know how much feeds through into 'lifetime wealth'?   If people have a bequest motive defined in terms of housing services, the increase in the value of their housing may not affect their spending at all.

In conclusion, one general point may be reiterated, which goes back to the danger of treating symptoms rather than underlying causes, and which has a crucial bearing on the policy qestion.   Suppose house prices are treated as a cause when in fact they should be treated as a symptom. Attempts to dampen demand by moderating house price inflation either through an income effect, or by a generalised interest rate increase, may indeed be successful.   Alternatively, a policy which is specifically targetted on the housing market may activate a substitution effect from housing into other forms of consumer spending and hence may be counterproductive.

5 Housing and labour market constraints on migration across the North-South divide

Ian Gordon

Introduction

Labour migration is, or has been, the crucial factor in the adjustment of regional labour markets to shifts in patterns of locational advantage within the United Kingdom. This can be seen clearly over the period between 1921 and 1971, when the balance of employment in Britain shifted decisively to the south. During this time employment growth in the regions of the north and west was some four million jobs short of that in the midlands and the south. Natural change in the working age population would have required similarly large increases in employment in each of these groups of regions, whereas the actual difference in growth rates over this 50–year period was about 40 per cent. Yet, at the end of that period, unemployment in all the regions of the north and west was under 5 per cent, while the north–south difference in unemployment rates was only 2 per cent. Since 1971, there has been a net loss of about 960,000 jobs in the north – an area in which the West Midlands now has to be included after the reversal of its economic fortunes – while about 920,000 jobs have been added to the southern regions (including the East Midlands). This represents a difference in rates of employment change of about 17 per cent (or 1 per cent per annum). The result in this case, however, involves a doubling of the gap in unemployment rates (which stood at 10.6 per cent in the north and 5.8 per cent in the south in mid–1988). In addition, there is now a wide disparity in participation rates, which in 1985 represented a north–south difference in concealed unemployment of 6.2 per cent (compared with 1.6 per cent in 1975). So far, at least,

75

labour migration appears to have been much less effective in equilibrating imbalances between the regional labour markets than it was in the period up to the late 1960s.

Why this should be so is an important question which seems to have a bearing on the efficiency of operation of the national labour market, and specifically on the vexed question of continuing wage inflation in the face of persistent high unemployment (Bover *et al.*, 1988). One answer could be that it is misleading to compare periods of such unequal length since adjustment through labour migration is a slow process. Much of the interregional shift in employment occurred during the depression of the 1920s and early 1930s, and the marked disparities in unemployment evident even in the late 1930s indicate that this was not entirely matched by movement of labour during those decades. However, if we take a period similar in length to 1971–88, we find that between 1951 and 1971 there was an 8 per cent north–south difference in employment growth rates, which appears to have been accommodated by migration within the period – since the gap in unemployment rates actually reduced slightly.

The impression that labour migration has in the past responded strongly and quite rapidly to interregional shifts in demand is borne out by some time–series analyses for particular regions spanning the period from the 1950s to the 1980s. A direct study of Scottish migration[1] indicated that in the period up to the late 1960s about 70 per cent of the effect of a demand shock to employment would be absorbed by migrational adjustments within three years. An indirect analysis using unemployment and employment data suggested that 80 per cent of such effects had been taken up by migration in this time (Gordon, 1985b). A similar analysis for Greater London, which is obviously a more accessible labour market, suggested that migrational adjustment in that period would have been more or less complete within the first year (Gordon, 1988). It thus appears to be the case that within recent memory labour migration functioned effectively as an adjustment mechanism but that this is no longer true. A central question here, in relation particularly to movement across the north–south divide, is why this change should have occurred – whether housing constraints can explain this shift, or whether the answer has to be sought elsewhere.

The inadequacy of regional migration in the 1980s has been more generally noted than its adequacy in earlier periods. Hence, while a range of explanations have been offered for low current levels of mobility, few of them address the question of why the efficiency of labour migration should have fallen. The most prominent of the arguments which have been canvassed all relate to housing market factors constraining individuals' ability to respond to labour market incentives for mobility. Four such hypotheses need to be considered:–

(i) that, for manual workers in particular, the existence of a more–or–less untransferable housing subsidy associated with tenancy of a local authority dwelling or other property with a controlled rent, offers a substantial disincentive to migration (Gleave and Palmer, 1979; Hughes and McCormick, 1981). Strong empirical support for this hypothesis has been provided (notably by Hughes and McCormick, 1987), although this does not extend to Minford *et al.*'s (1988) speculative extrapolations of the implications for regional and national unemployment (see following section). With the exception of a few years in the mid 1960s, when it was relaxed, this mobility constraint has operated at a broadly comparable level since at least the late 1950s (Bover *et al.*, 1988), and does not therefore appear a likely explanation of the weakening of mobility in the 1970s and 1980s.

(ii) that, particularly for white collar workers, mobility to areas of high labour demand is discouraged in periods when widening regional differentials in house–price/earnings ratios reduce the prospective gains from such a move in real income terms. Muellbauer and Murphy (1988a) seem to have shown that this factor is of central importance for net migration to the south–east. However, it is not clear that labour migration (in the sense of combined workplace and residence moves) to the region is substantially affected, nor that this factor is significant in relation to moves across the north–south divide (see third section below). In any case, its relevance is relatively short–term (though short–term constraints on labour market adjustment may have damaging long–term consequences), and it has been specifically used to explain net out–migration from the south–east in the early 1970s and mid–1980s, rather than any downward shift in, or continuing constraint on, labour mobility.

(iii) that, for other owner–occupiers, seeking to move away from the regions of high labour and housing demand, such boom periods may discourage migration because they seem to imply a continued divergence in regional house prices, and hence the loss of prospective investment gains if they move. This argument (also discussed by Muellbauer and Murphy, 1988) would help, alongside the preceding hypothesis, to explain a reduction in gross (as distinct from net) migration during the mid–1980s, which might also have detrimental economic effects, although not in relation to the north–south divide. It is not clear, however, why similar evidence should lead immigrants to the south to be discouraged by high house price levels (ignoring prospective capital gains), while potential emigrants remain attracted by house price inflation (ignoring cost of living effects) – and a mirror–image scenario seems just as plausible. In any case, it is questionable whether the average home owner does, or should, assume the continuance of divergent rates of inflation beyond the short term. Casual empiricism, reported in various recent sources, suggests that a number of home owners do in fact believe this, but such observations may only reflect a predictable increase in the variance of expectations about future price changes. Econometric support for this hypothesis is lacking so far, and Muellbauer's results for outflows from the south–east clearly support hypothesis (ii) as against this alternative, with rising house prices in the region increasing rates of emigration.

(iv) that, particularly for younger workers and/or manual groups for whom owner–occupation is less attractive or feasible, mobility has been constrained by the shrinking stock of private accommodation available for rent, in the face of both rent controls and continuing tax subsidies to owner occupation (Gleave and Palmer, 1979). Certainly this sector still plays a strong role in interregional migration, accommodating 30 per cent of economically active migrants from the north to the south in 1984. And it is also the case that the decline in this sector was particularly fast during the 1960s (falling from 32 per cent of the stock in 1960 to 25 per cent in 1965, 20 per cent in 1970 – and then to 13 per cent in 1980 and 10 per cent in 1986). Migrants may have been less than proportionately affected by this contraction, for example, because more of them are to be found in the furnished part of the sector, which has not been so severely cut back. Nevertheless, this is the one housing market factor which could have contributed significantly to a secular reduction in the effectiveness of labour migration.

Regional unemployment and the required rate of labour migration

If the proposition is that the current level of labour migration is inadequate, it may be useful to start by considering whether the shortfall can be quantified. In fact there are two quite different approaches to this question, based on contrasting assumptions about the degree of integration or segmentation of the labour market within any area. On the one hand, if there is a high degree of integration across occupational and industrial sub-markets, the role of labour mobility may be seen simply in terms of shifting units of labour from areas of absolute or relative excess supply to areas of absolute or relative excess demand. In this case what matters is net migration, and required levels of mobility can be fairly simply quantified. This remains the case if the labour market is seen as consisting of a finite number of discrete and empirically separable sub-markets. If, on the other hand, the market is conceived of as highly differentiated, being made up of a heterogeneous collection of specific jobs, then what is relevant would be the level of gross migration between regions, with there being no simple measure of adequacy. Popular discussion of the 'mobility problem' has at various times reflected both of these models, sometimes focussing on the need for migration out of the north to relieve unemployment levels, and at other times on the problems of filling specific vacancies, in the north as well as the south, either through the internal or the external labour market. Neither model is obviously inappropriate, but in relation to the north–south divide, on which this chapter focusses, the first approach is clearly more relevant.

From this aggregative, or integrated, perspective, a natural measure of the required rate of net migration to or from an area is that which would be required to maintain a constant difference in unemployment rates in relation to the average for the migrational system (for example, the nation).[2] A more demanding alternative criterion clearly could be that net migration is sufficient to eliminate such unemployment differentials, but the parallelism criterion is a simpler starting point, both analytically and empirically. For a two–region system (with areas sufficiently large and well defined to make commuting flows insignificant) the required rate of labour migration is then given by:

$$m_i{}^* = (r_i - \bar{r}) - (s_i - \bar{s}) - \Delta p_i - \Delta \bar{p}) \tag{1}$$

where $m_i{}^*$ = the required rate of net labour migration to region i; r = the rate of employment growth; s = the rate of natural change in labour supply; Δp = the rate of participation change; bars denote average values for the regional system; and all rates are expressed in relation to a common denominator (the economically active population at time t). If differential trends in participation rates are regarded as reflections of variations in concealed unemployment, and the rates of open plus hidden unemployment are required to move in parallel, the third bracketed term drops out of this equation, making the required rate of migration a simple function of differences in employment growth and natural change in labour supply.

The equilibrium regional unemployment rate model, suggested originally by Brown (1972), shows that this required rate of labour migration will be achieved in practice so long as migrants respond to levels of unemployment in prospective origin and/or destination areas, whether directly or perhaps indirectly through the mediating effect of wage variations (Burridge and Gordon, 1981). If this migrational response is instantaneous, the required rate of labour migration will always be achieved, and regional unemployment rates will move in parallel, until there is some shift in relative rates of employment growth and/or natural change in labour supply. If, alternatively, there is a discrete lag in the response of migrants to regional unemployment, actual rates of labour migration will be a positive function of past rates of required migration, such that if the rate of required migration fluctuates only randomly the actual rate of migration will move towards its mean asymptotically. How fast it approaches this target would depend both upon the length of the lag and upon the strength of the migrational response to unemployment, but the required rate will eventually be achieved and may be approximated quite closely within a few years. The circumstances in which it is achieved may vary markedly, however, since if the migrational response is weak it will require a proportionately larger difference in unemployment rates as an incentive before the required rate of migration is achieved.

To express this a little more clearly, a simple model can be set up in which net migration is related to differences in current rates of employment change and in a lagged unemployment rate:

$$m_{it} = \psi(\alpha(r_i - \bar{r})t - \beta(u_i - \bar{u})_{t-\lambda}) \tag{2}$$

where u = the unemployment rate.
When the lag (λ) is zero, net migration will occur at the required rate, with a differential unemployment rate given by:

$$(u_i - \bar{u}) = (1/\psi\beta)[(s_i - \bar{s}) - (1 - \psi\alpha)(r_i - \bar{r})] \tag{3}$$

It can be seen that the unemployment differential associated with faster or slower rates of employment growth depends upon the responsiveness of migration to unemployment and employment growth differences (through the α and β parameters), and that any general influences on the mobility level (via ψ) will have an inversely proportional effect on unemployment differentials. For any sub-market category, region or time period in which rates of mobility are only (say) half the norm, unemployment differences would be twice what would otherwise be expected. (With positive lags the same solution is reached in the long run, provided that the employment and supply growth rates are constant.)

One conclusion to be drawn from this argument is that the relationship between actual and required rates of movement is not a sufficient indicator of the efficiency of labour migration. If actual movement falls short of the required level for more than the odd year or two, this is evidence of a problem going beyond a simple lag in response. However, the achievement of the required rate of migration over a long period of time may not indicate an absence of serious constraint on movement, if it is accompanied by a substantial disparity in unemployment rates.[3]

The simple model outlined above can be used as a rather more straightforward basis for investigating the possible effects of interregional differences in housing tenure constraints on unemployment than the equilibrium model presented by Minford *et al.*(1988). Although the latter was estimated on mixed cross-section/time-series data, the degree of autocorrelation is such that few of the temporal observations are independent, and their housing tenure variable explains none of the change over time. What is offered as evidence of a significant effect of mobility constraints on unemployment thus depends essentially on a cross-regional analysis with few degrees of freedom. The specification of the demand side of their model can be criticised for ignoring any sources of cost variation other than local authority rates, which are clearly a minor item, for ignoring the interaction between different regional industrial mixes and inter-industry differences in technical progress or capital-labour substitution, as well as the substantial variations in output growth rates within the manufacturing sector. However, the limited number of degrees of freedom available in a cross-regional analysis can scarcely justify attempts at a more appropriate specification of the demand side of their model. A simpler approach may therefore be appropriate, taking the employment change as given and seeking to examine how its effects on unemployment are mediated by factors affecting the responsiveness of migration.

In the case of the controlled sectors of the housing market the conventional argument about untransferable subsidies only appears to be relevant to expected rates of emigration from specific regions (rather than inflows). In regions where more of the population enjoy such subsidies, the rate of emigration (gross and net) should be both lower and less responsive to the relative level of regional unemployment: in consequence these regions should have equilibrium rates of unemployment which are both higher (in all cases) and more responsive to differential rates of employment (or labour supply) change.[4] There are, however, some other factors which are likely to reduce the responsiveness of labour migration (and hence increase that of unemployment) in particular regions. In particular, less accessible (that is, larger and more remote) regions should be generally less open to migrational flows. Also, for reasons discussed in the next section, job losses are expected to give rise to proportionately smaller migrational responses than job gains; thus for a given net change in jobs, unemployment is likely to be higher where there have been more (gross) job losses.

A fairly basic model of demand deficient unemployment might thus take the form:

$$u_i = a_0 + a_1 MOBIL + a_2 JLOSS + a_3 JGAIN + a_4 JLOSS*MOBIL + a_5 JGAIN*MOBIL$$
$$+ a_6 ACCESS*JLOSS + a_7 ACCESS*JGAIN$$

where MOBIL = a tenure based indicator of potential mobility; JLOSS = proportionate rate of job losses; JGAIN = proportionate rate of job gains; ACCESS = accessibility in terms of population potential.
The number of parameters involved, even when all structural characteristics are excluded, is too large for sensible estimation across eleven standard regions. However, a series of analyses using data for unemployment in 1971 (in the middle of Minford's series) and for employment gains and losses in the previous decade, from Law (1980), yielded no significant evidence of a mobility effect. Rather, the best parsimonious model involved only the rate of job loss and its interaction with regional accessibility. Further work is required across a more disaggregated set of areas, but these preliminary results suggest that Minford *et al.*'s (1988) results suggesting a strong connection between regional unemployment and the housing tenure mix should be viewed with extreme scepticism.

North–south migrational flows

The main geographical imbalance in the United Kingdom labour market lies between the regions of the north and those of the south, with the former group having an unemployment rate about two thirds above the latter. The position of the East Midlands in relation to this divide is a little ambiguous (Green, 1988) but the southern parts of the region are particularly strongly tied to the labour markets of the south–east and these links are the largest element in the region's migrational flows. Including the East Midlands in the south, with East Anglia, the south–west and the south–east, and assigning all other regions to the 'north', isolates a set of north–south flows which are primarily associated with moves for job reasons, unlike the interregional flows within the south. According to the 1985 Labour Force Survey (LFS), 72 per cent of economically active male migrants between north and south made moves for job reasons, which were responsible for all of the net shift from north to south. (By contrast the net outflow observed for the south–east standard region on its own was entirely attributable to non–job reasons.) Dividing the country in this way yields two meta–regions of virtually identical size in terms of employment, which are sufficiently self–contained for unambiguous comparisons to be made of the relationship between employment, unemployment, and migrational shifts.

As a point of departure we can make an estimate of the 'required' level of north–south migration by subtracting the differential in employment growth rates from that in natural change of labour supply, and then dividing by the typical proportion of economically active people among north–south migrants. For a point estimate of the labour supply growth rates, we may look at the difference between the 16–20 and 60–64 age cohorts in the 1981 Census, which implies a working age population in the north growing (in the absence of migration) at 0.08 per cent per annum above the national average – requiring the emigration of 11,000 economically active persons to offset it. Adding to this, a rate of employment decline in the north running at about 54,000 jobs per annum above the national average over the 1971–88 period, yields a required net migration rate from north to south of around 64,000 economically active people. Data from the OPCS Longitudinal Study linking 1971 and 1981 Census records suggests that the effective participation rate among net north–south migrants has been about 68 per cent. Hence the required rate of overall net migration in this period would have been about 94,000 a year. This is about twice the actual rate of movement, of some 38,000 a year, according to NHSCR sources.[5]

For the previous twenty–year period (1951–71) similar calculations suggest a required rate of migration of about 74,000 per annum, against observed gains from all forms of migration of 54,000 in the south and losses of 69,000 in the north (Law, 1980). As compared with this period of approximate balance, actual migration appears to have significantly slowed in the 1970s and 1980s, while the required level of movement has significantly increased. Within these past two decades, however, there has been a considerable variation in experience. Between 1972 and 1977 for example, the north–south gap in employment change was cut back to about 5,000 jobs a year, and while the level of net migration was also substantially reduced it seems to have been at around its required level. In the late 1970s, however, the gap in employment trends reopened, with the differential widening sharply in the post–1979 recession, to a peak of 152,000 jobs in 1980–81 and an average of 98,000 a year over the 1980–85 period. There was some increase in net migration to the south, but in the years 1978–85 this remained fairly flat, with the balance varying between 45,000 and 57,000 movers, against required numbers of about 159,000 per annum. Since 1985, however, when the difference in employment change has fallen back to 54,000 per annum (as in 1977–9) there seems to have been a marked increase in net migration to the south (which in the two years up to the third quarter of 1987) is running at around 70,000 per annum.

This picture of changing migrational trends from north to south differs in some respects from the pattern for the south–east alone (analysed by Muellbauer and Murphy, 1988). One obvious difference is that the south–east region was a net exporter of migrants throughout the 1970s, and again since 1985, whereas the south as a whole had gains in almost every year. A second and more crucial difference is that whereas the south–east region reverted to net losses after 1984 with a particularly large net outflow in 1987 (almost equal to those in 1972 and 1973), the south as a whole has had its largest net inflows in the past two years (quite the reverse of its experience in 1973). The difference between these two series[6] essentially reflects the rate of decentralisation of population within the south, and it closely parallels the changing rate of net outflow from London to other parts of the south–east. Since it is this intra–south movement which is liable to be most sensitive to housing rather than labour market factors, it is not perhaps surprising to find that between 1982 and 1986, when relative house prices in the south–east were rising sharply, the region's gains from the north increased markedly (from 26,000 to 42,000) while its losses to the rest of the south also grew (from 22,000 to 45,000). This sharp contrast in a key period for the analysis of house price effects suggests that Muellbauer and Murphy's (1988) conclusions about their central role in influencing migrational flows to and from the south–east probably do not apply to north–south moves, and hence may have limited relevance to the main geographical imbalances in the labour market. Indeed other studies which have attempted to separate interregional labour migration from housing related moves have found house prices exerting a fairly minor influence on the former (Molho, 1984; Gordon, 1982; Molho and Gordon, 1987).

Such a negative conclusion, however, obviously leaves open the question of how we are to explain fluctuations in the level of north–south movement, and in its efficiency as a labour market equilibrator. The other significant variables in Muellbauer and Murphy's results which may be more relevant to the longer distance flows are: an index of potential constraints associated with controlled housing tenures; the rate of relative employment growth, the unemployment rate differential; relative non–manual earnings in the south–east; and changes in the balance of international migration. The last of these factors probably functions as a stimulant to decentralisation within the south, since a disproportionate share of international flows came to or from London.[7] Of the other factors cited, relative employment growth and unemployment rates would both have implied a substantial increase in north–south migration during the recession of the early 1980s, while trends in the nominal earnings differential would have predicted a continuing growth in the flow since 1981. Against these strengthening incentives for movement, the burden of explaining the inelasticity of migration during the early 1980s apparently falls on the tenure variable which reaches its lowest point in 1982 (having fallen sharply since 1979).

An alternative explanation for the diminished effectiveness of labour migration, advanced in Gordon (1985a and b), focusses on the influence of macroeconomic factors on the willingness and ability of workers to undertake the significant act of investment in human capital involved in long distance migration. These factors were seen as affecting the financial resources of migrants, the perceived uncertainty attached to gains from undertaking moves to an unfamiliar environment, and the likelihood of receiving information about distant job opportunities. The national unemployment rate was taken as a simple index of the relevant macroeconomic conditions, and evidence was produced in relation to Scottish migrational flows that higher general unemployment rates substantially curtailed the level of responsiveness of labour migration. Time–series estimates suggested that a doubling of male unemployment rates from the 2 per cent or so common in the 1960s to the 5 per cent level reached in the mid–1970s would have reduced mobility by almost two thirds. However, they also suggested that after unemployment passed 5 or 6 per cent further increases, such as those experienced in the late 1970s and 1980s, should have had little additional effect in depressing mobility.

For a labour market explanation of the particular ineffectiveness of migration in responding to the great north–south gap in rates of employment change which opened up between 1979 and 1981, we have to look beyond the effects of a generally slack labour market to the particular manner in which this gap emerged. Essentially it was a result of accelerating manufacturing job losses in the north, with most of the difference in net employment change taking the form of higher rates of redundancy as compared with the south. Such involuntary job losses are much less likely to stimulate emigration from a region than new job creation is to stimulate immigration, since redundancies create no new opportunities for movement, and any migratory response depends largely on the initiative of the particular person who happens to become unemployed. By contrast service job increases, such as those in the south in the mid–1980s are especially liable to stimulate in–migration (Gordon, 1988). If the initial job change does not create a migratory response, then everything depends on the secondary incentive provided by the widening gap in unemployment (and perhaps in wages) caused by the shortfall of actual from required migratory shifts. The north–south unemployment gap did indeed widen markedly between 1979 and 1981. Since then, however, despite a continuing shortfall in out–migration, the gap has remained virtually unchanged and the growing excess supply of workers in the north has been diverted out of the labour market into early retirement and other forms of economic inactivity. Such ex–workers are no longer candidates for labour migration, and their growing numbers provide no reason for anybody else to leave the region (in contrast to a circulating chance of becoming unemployed). A further consideration is that long or repeated spells of unemployment tend to worsen workers' competitive position in the labour market, converting demand deficient into structural unemployment, for which migration is no solution.

The problem of manual worker mobility

On two counts it would appear that the problem of unresponsiveness of labour migration in the 1980s is principally one relating to manual workers. In the first place, they account for at least two thirds of the unemployed. More specifically, however, it was the manufacturing job losses of the north in the early 1980s which failed to stimulate a migratory response comparable with that apparently generated by differential rates of service job growth. Analyses of sample data from the Labour Force Surveys suggests that, since the mid–1970s, there has been no significant net movement of manual workers from north to south, in contrast to the higher non–manual groups. The 1985 survey suggests that a reason for this lack of net migration is a northward drift of people (possibly return migrants) for non–job reasons, offsetting a modest southward flow of job movers. Overall, the likelihood of a non–manual worker moving from the north to the south is five times that of a manual worker's chances of making the same move, despite the fact that regional differences in labour market conditions are substantially greater in manual occupations. This gap appears to have widened substantially during the 1970s and 1980s. Data from the 1966 Census, for example, shows manual workers then accounting for about one third of the net flow from north to south. In the case of the northern region, 2.9 per cent of non–manual workers were recorded as leaving the region for other parts of Britain in 1965–6, compared with 1.0 per cent of manual workers; in 1980–81 a slightly lower rate was recorded for the non–manual group (2.5 per cent) but the rate of manual emigration had fallen by two fifths (to 0.6 per cent). In this instance at least, most of the reduction in mobility seems to have been among manual workers.

Evidence from the 1984 LFS indicates that among manual workers, as among their non–manual counterparts, public sector tenants, and those who own their properties outright, are only half as likely to move south as are those with current mortgages, while private sector tenants are many times more likely to do so. This simply confirms for this particular group of long distance migrants what Hughes and McCormick (Chapter 6) have shown for all job related movers, and it raises the same questions as to how far the differences reflect self–selection of tenure groups in relation to expected mobility, and how far the housing tenure actually causes differences in mobility. In the case of private tenants, self–selection is likely to be a major factor, a view which is supported by Hughes and McCormick's (1985) analysis of expressed wishes to make an interregional move. This analysis suggested, however, that there was no significant difference between public renters and owner–occupiers in the desire for such a move when other relevant factors had been controlled for, implying that the difference in actual movement was essentially a reflection of the constraints on those in the public sector. However, it has to be borne in mind that, in the presence of constraint, the numbers wanting to make a move represent the stock of those who have been frustrated, whereas the actual moves represent a flow. In this situation an equal proportion of aspirant movers among council tenants and owner occupiers would imply some degree of self–selection against potential movers in recruitment to the public sector. Hence the relative odds of actual movement in the two sectors probably overstate the effect of the tenure variable.

The fact that mobility is comparably low among outright owners and council tenants, even when age differences are controlled for, raises other questions. In this case a different form of self–selection may be involved, since a longer length of residence is characteristic of the outright owners, who are thus likely to include more of the generally immobile as well as those who have become attached to a particular property and area. But it may be significant that outright owners and council tenants also share roughly double the chances, as compared to mortgagors, of becoming unemployed. Hughes and McCormick have suggested that this differential may reflect a weaker financial incentive to seek work. Jenkins' (1986) examination of recruitment practices suggests that personnel officers share some such view, preferring workers with 'a wife, two kids and a mortgage round their necks'. Similar arguments may be relevant to the propensity to move for job reasons. Either debt itself may be a positive incentive to undertaking search for employment over a wider field, or mortgagors may have a greater chance of successfully completing such a search and organising a move on a contracted rather than speculative basis.

Even taking the lower rate of movement in the public sector (though not among outright owners) as a pure expression of constraint, it can explain only a small part of the manual/non–manual difference in migration rates. With about half of northern manual workers in the public sector, their wholesale transfer to mortgaged owner–occupation would only raise the level of north–south movement by around 50 per cent. Even manual workers with mortgages are three times or so less likely to move from the north to the south than the average non–manual worker, or than their counterparts in the United States (Hughes and McCormick, 1988).

For many non–manual workers, long distance job movement is eased by essentially national information networks, the possession of generally recognised qualifications, employer interest in longer term job attachments and the fact that demand is growing, offering a constant stream of new job vacancies. For most manual workers these conditions do not apply, even to the skilled, in recruiting when employers may make particular use of the qualitative information, and control, offered by informal (and hence localised) modes of recruitment. High levels of unemployment over the past decade or so have exacerbated this difference. Hence manual workers in a high unemployment region who may contemplate migration are faced with the choice between seeking a stable and secure job, which they may be as likely to achieve near at hand, or making a speculative move to search and take whatever is available. The latter course is risky and potentially costly, especially in a situation where little rented accommodation is available on the open market. Access to secure employment through such speculative migration may well be particularly difficult in a context where immobility has become the norm, and a sign of stability, among manual workers.

The situation is obviously somewhat different for the unemployed, who are twice as likely as otherwise similar workers to make north–south moves. However, even for this group it must be very difficult to judge at what point in a spell it becomes worthwhile, between the early phases when chances of local re–employment seem high, and later stages when financial resources are strained and the chance of work anywhere has fallen. The potential loss of local sources of financial and psychic support must also be a deterrent to movement for the unemployed. In any event their contribution to actual shifts of labour supply has always been low, at least in the postwar period. Thus the achievement of required levels of labour migration depends essentially on movements of workers in employment responding to better opportunities elsewhere of which they have become aware. The apparent lack of such opportunities for most manual workers in Britain during the 1980s, combined with the difficulty of access to short–term rented accommodation which discourages speculative moves, are the most likely explanations for the disappearance of any drift to the south among manual workers.

Conclusion

Recent debates have offered two hypotheses to account for the apparent ineffectiveness of continuing high levels of unemployment as a means of checking wage inflation. One of these emphasises the role of structural constraints in the labour market which serve to separate an increasing proportion of the unemployed from the main arenas in which bargains are struck and hirings made. The second hypothesis emphasises the importance of impediments to spatial adjustment in the labour market, arising particularly from the workings of the housing system.

The contention of this chapter is that, while interregional labour migration does appear to have become markedly less efficient, particularly since the late 1970s, housing constraints are an unlikely explanation for that change. Over a longer period, the shrinking availability of private rented accommodation, especially in growing areas outside the cities, is likely to have been an increasingly important constraint on movement. The element of tied subsidy in the controlled rental sector must also have been important, although this may have diminished rather than increased over the past decade. But both of these factors would also have operated strongly in the 1960s and early 1970s when interregional labour migration appears to have been an efficient adjustment mechanism. Nor does there seem to be any real evidence that recent house price inflation has significantly inhibited north–south moves, however much it may have stimulated residential moves within the south.

The alternative view argued here is that labour, rather than housing, market factors are likely to have been responsible for the curtailment of labour migration in the 1980s – or rather for its failure to achieve the higher levels of net migration required in the face of a wider disparity in rates of employment change. To start with, it has been found that high levels of unemployment serve to generally depress mobility. Over and above this effect, however, it is argued that the structural impediments to labour market adjustment serve also to inhibit spatial adjustment in the market. In particular the same processes which make it harder for redundant workers in any region to regain secure employment also reduce the chances of the necessary out–migration being generated from regions which have borne the brunt of job loss in the 1980s.

Geographical mobility of labour is vitally important to the efficient operation of national labour markets, and the operation of the housing system is, as Hughes, McCormick, Minford and others have contended, an important constraint on such mobility. From this point of view, steps to secure more rentable stock accessible to long distance migrants and to break the link between housing subsidy and occupancy of particular properties would be very welcome. Such steps might also contribute in some degree to reducing the apparent discrimination against public sector tenants (or in favour of mortgagors) in competition for jobs. However, it would be a great mistake to pin responsibility for the ineffectiveness of labour migration as an adjustment mechanism during the 1980s (in contrast to the experience of the 1960s) – or still more for the upward drift of the NAIRU (i.e. the rate of unemployment that would maintain a constant rate of inflation) – on the constraining effect of housing. In both cases the major impediments need to be sought within the labour market itself.

Notes

1   Assuming proportionality between the balance of total and economically active migrant flows.
2   In a multiregional system, this average needs to be weighted towards the nearer regions with which the area has stronger migrational relations – although if all regions exhibit the required rate of net migration as defined on this basis, then all unemployment rates will move in parallel, and the question of weighting will become irrelevant.
3   The point is made cautiously since there may be a significant structural element to such unemployment differentials, which labour migration, however efficient, would not serve to reduce (Gordon, 1987).
4   Minford *et al.* assume that such housing constraints would only affect migration (and thereby unemployment) in the regions with net out–migration, a group which actually includes the south–east although it is a gainer from labour migration.
5   The shortfall may be exaggerated here because the actual migration figures relate only to domestic migration, whereas some of the required migration may be achieved through higher rates of overseas emigration from the declining regions.
6   Or between the south–east's own series and its expected share of

north–south flows (about 60 per cent).

7   It may also be the case, however, that during the recession period of the early 1980s, when prospects anywhere in Britain were particularly poor, international emigration served as a substitute for north–south migration.

Comment on Chapter 5

Moira Munro

Gordon, in this chapter, does several useful things.   First, he places recent migration trends into a longer perspective, which provides a context in which to evaluate the impact of housing market constraints on labour market mobility.   Second, he provides some estimates of the desired levels of mobility: something that has been neglected, although it is implicit in and crucial to much of the debate in this area. Finally, he discusses the problem of the low mobility of manual workers and provides a re–examination of the importance of the housing system in determining the overall levels of mobility within this sector.   This comment will examine these three elements of the chapter in turn, but the argument for the incorporation of 'micro–foundations' into the discussion of these issues will provide a unifying theme.

First, the discussion of the impact of the housing system on labour market mobility is refreshing.   It takes a more measured view of the likely barrier to labour mobility constituted by the housing system.   The conventional wisdom can be characterised as casting housing markets as the chief offender in preventing the smooth operation of labour markets, through the substantial administrative, financial and accessibility barriers which discourage longer–distance mobility, both within and between tenures (a view strongly propounded by Minford *et al.*, 1987, and reflected in much 'popular' discussion of the subject).   It would be expected that the welfare losses resulting from the exogenous constraints to interregional labour market moves are significant; there are likely to be considerable welfare losses at the individual level (as there is an increased likelihood of suffering unnecessarily lengthy periods of unemployment and the consequent losses in earnings, skills and so on), there will also be productivity and growth losses to firms and hence a slower growth in national income and, furthermore, the housing sector has been argued to be part of the reason for the continued, perverse association of high unemployment with relatively high wages and wage inflation.   Long–distance mobility and the operation of the housing sector is therefore seen as a major issue in the efficiency of the national economy.

However, the argument that is made in this chapter is that the role of housing has been overstated: there has been a substantial decline in the rates of labour market mobility that cannot be explained by equivalent changes in the conditions that operate within the housing market. This is argued to be most important in relation to the local authority housing sector where the policy of maintaining relatively low rents has been sustained over a long period. While this point appears to be valid when considering the local authority rental sector in isolation, proof would have to rest on an analysis which took into account the changing relative size of the sector and the role that it plays in housing the population. For instance, the recent debate on 'residualisation' has highlighted the longer–term changes (say, over the last twenty years) in the characteristics of local authority tenants. In particular, tenants of the local authority have become increasingly concentrated among the least advantaged in labour market terms and increasingly dependent on welfare benefits (see Hamnett and Randolf, 1988). Thus it would be wrong to assume that council housing played the same role in the longer term, as the changes in the population outlined above might lead, amongst other things, to an expectation of reduced average propensities for long distance mobility to be observed over time among local authority tenants.

The second element of the constraint on labour market clearing exerted by housing markets is that of the marked price differences between low and high priced regions which are argued both to discourage migration to the high priced regions (because of the high cost of housing) and to discourage migrants *from* high priced regions who fear the loss of their place on the housing ladder in the more expensive area. Gordon rightly points to the contradictory elements contained here: the same price differential is postulated to have quite opposite effects on two groups of potential movers. However, the apparent contradiction is probably reduced when the discussion is couched more in terms of absolute differences in the levels of prices. It may be that some potential migrants simply could not afford to buy in the more expensive parts of the country, even if the wage earned were greater than in their origin region (even where a 'London weighting' is given, it may not always reflect the true difference in the cost of living in the south–east). Hence, given capital market and affordability constraints, the owner–occupied sector may remain a barrier to mobility even though all may prefer access to the higher capital gain/wealth accumulation possibilities of high priced regions. Ultimately, the importance of the price barrier to mobility from either side of such a divide may be revealed only in a detailed, micro (household based) study which allowed an examination of the constraints that face individuals attempting a long–distance, labour–market move, the expected and actual costs that they face in undertaking a move and the expected and actual benefits (or disbenefits) from changes in living standards, quality of life, work conditions and wages.

The second element of the chapter is the estimation of desired rates of mobility. It is very welcome to see the desired rates of (net) mobility explicitly derived from a desired pattern of (equilibrium) employment and unemployment through the country (here postulated to be the maintenance of constant differentials between the rates of unemployment in different parts of the country). It is also an approach which recognises the dynamic nature of the issue of housing and labour market clearing and hence is able to discuss the difference between a temporary and a longer–term disequilibrium. Although the exact nature of an 'optimal' pattern is clearly somewhat arbitrarily decided, in the absence of an explicit benchmark, discussion has often centred round an inadequately defined problem of 'constrained' and 'insufficient' mobility (or rested on simplistic comparisons of the United Kingdom with other countries). A closely related issue, although outside the scope of the chapter, is whether, having defined the desired pattern of unemployment, the process of labour mobility should be expected to bear all the brunt of the achievement of this end. In particular, the approach implicitly takes the demand for labour as a given, rather than as a parameter of the problem. Hence there is no scope for a potential *employers*' response of locating in areas of higher unemployment as a major equilibrating mechanism. This is a consequence of the conceptualisation of the problem as one of 'labour mobility' rather than 'the distribution of employment'.

The final element in Gordon's chapter is an interesting discussion of the problem of low mobility amongst manual workers in particular. The starting point for this discussion is that manual workers have been particularly affected by the job losses in the north, which have been concentrated in the manufacturing sector. The discussion emphasises that housing is only one of a number of factors that might contribute to the observed lack of mobility among these workers. There are two comments that may be made in relation to this discussion.

First, there is only passing reference in the discussion to the uncertainties involved in making a long–distance move. These uncertainties relate to the outcomes of a wide range of factors relating to job (conditions, prospects, colleagues and so on), housing and social connections (including schools for children, the possibility of establishing new social networks, proximity to family and so on through a very broad range of potential problems of re–establishment). These uncertainties bear emphasising for two reasons. First in relation to housing, although giving up a house in the origin region will always be risky, there is increased risk for council tenants who face less prospect of being able to return to equivalent accommodation if they wish (because of the administrative rules which govern the allocation of council housing which seldom give priority to in–migrants). Second, the uncertainty can be managed much better in more affluent households. The possibility of rectifying a mistake, either by relocating within the new area, or even returning to the origin area, or the capacity to make smaller adjustments in terms of maintaining or developing social contacts, is to a large extent dependent on income. Hence the risk involved in making a long–distance move is likely to be greater for poorer people. Manual workers are likely to be poorer than non–manual workers and hence the resources for coping with such risks are less. Consequently, it would be predicted that manual workers will need relatively greater compensation for undertaking a move in order to offset the greater risk.

This argument is related to the second point that will be made concerning the problems of mobility among manual workers. Gordon identifies no satisfactory explanation for the Hughes and McCormick (1981) finding that, although council tenants have a lower propensity to migrate than do owner–occupiers, outright owners actually have the lowest mobility rates of all. One hypothesis that seems plausible relates to the adequacy of the *ceteris paribus* assumption, when comparing the mobility of owner occupiers, private tenants and public tenants. Although in a subsequent paper Hughes and McCormick (1985) tested the hypothesis that there were differences in intentions to move, an equally important question would seem to be whether the lack of an income variable conceals a violation of the *ceteris paribus* assumption. Their earlier paper (1981) reports the inclusion of an income variable in some early regression analysis that proves to be insignificant, although they recognise that the measure they use may not be totally appropriate. Clearly SEG bears a fairly close relationship to income, but it could be argued that tenure is itself a better possible proxy. The advantages that are perceived to accrue to owner occupiers (both financial, in terms of rates of return and wealth accumulation, and social, such as increased freedom and independence) are now so commonly believed to be very significant that it would seem likely that a great proportion of people who can afford to do so now own a house. This will have become increasingly the case as the 'Right–to–Buy' has allowed the more affluent local authority tenants, who are satisfied with their accommodation, to buy their council house (at a discounted price). Hence, when comparing a group of manual workers who are owner occcupiers with a group of manual workers who are council tenants, it is probable that the former group are richer (both in current income terms and probably also in having a greater amount of accumulated savings) than the latter. Outright owners, on the other hand, fall mainly into two categories; older people who have paid off their mortgage and a group of people who pay with cash for houses (possibly supplemented with informal or familial loans) because they are unable to gain access to capital markets or because the properties which they wish to buy are considered unsuitably high risk for the formal lending agencies (and the properties are typically cheap and in poor condition). For instance, Karn *et al.* (1985) found that ethnic minority groups were frequently outright owners of properties in very poor condition in inner city locations and argued that they were a very disadvantaged group with very few housing options. It is likely then, that a group of manual worker, outright owners would be poorer than an otherwise similar group of mortgaged owners. The comparison with council tenants is more difficult to predict, but there is no reason to suppose that outright owners would be systematically more favoured than council tenants.

If such an income (and/or wealth) difference exists between tenures (and it seems likely that it should) then this will go part of the way towards explaining the differential rates of household mobility in different tenures. For, as this chapter argues, resources are needed to undertake a long–distance move. The extra burden of uncertainty and risk borne by poorer people will act as an additional disincentive. If this argument is accepted, it becomes increasingly plausible that manual workers in council tenancies, or owning outright, would very seldom be given a labour market offer that would compensate them for the costs and risks of moving. Once again, it is necessary to establish whether this is indeed the case in a 'micro', household–based approach that examines the decision–making processes of potential and actual migrants in the different tenure groups.

In summary then, Gordon provides a useful way into the identification of the 'desired' level of mobility and gives a needed debunking of some of the 'taken for granted' elements of the commonly espoused arguments that blame labour market immobility on housing market constraints. It raises the possibility that labour market processes can themselves explain the apparently diminishing ability of the labour market to adjust to recent structural and recession determined changes in the labour market. Many of the questions raised here are worthy of further investigation, but it may be that more detailed evidence on individual choice and decision processes, especially in the light of the great uncertainty surrounding long–distance mobility, will be needed to illuminate the comparative 'height' of the housing barrier that faces different groups of potential long–distance labour market movers.

6 Housing and labour market mobility

G. A. Hughes and B. McCormick

Over the last eight years we have written a sequence of papers (see Hughes and McCormick, 1981, 1985, 1987) which have examined various aspects of the relationship between the housing market and the labour market in Britain with specific attention to the role of migration. In this chapter we will attempt first of all to summarise the stylised facts about this relationship. Then we will provide an overall interpretation of the impact of housing policies in shaping the manner in which the labour market responds to exogenous shocks.

Stylised facts

Before considering the main empirical results it is important to appreciate the nature of the data on which our findings rest. The crucial point is that we have relied upon large cross–section datasets (from the General Household Survey for 1973 and 1974 and the Labour Force Survey for 1981 and 1983–6). The advantage of cross–section data is that it enables one to identify important differences in behaviour between different segments of the labour force but this is achieved at some cost in terms of a loss of information about the impact of aggregate variables (for example, total unemployment, real wages, house prices) on the labour market. In our recent work we have attempted to surmount this problem by pooling data from surveys carried out in several years and by making use of regional and occupational differences in these aggregate variables. Inevitably, it is possible to point to potential technical problems which might affect the results. In particular, it can be argued that there may be a problem of simultaneity between migration, unemployment, wages and house prices at a regional level. We accept that it is not possible to discount such problems altogether but, as shown below, the gains from disaggregation are very large and our models have been designed to minimise the likelihood of specification errors.

A second feature of our work is that we have tended to concentrate on the decisions of heads of household (HoH) aged between 21 and 65 (59 for women) who are members of the labour force. This reflects a focus on labour market adjustment for a stable working population rather than on population flows. There are three groups which are excluded from the sample on this basis:

(i) Non–heads of household: With respect to migration behaviour these are, as one might expect, very similar to heads of household. There are some interesting differences between heads and non–heads of household with respect to decisions affecting participation in the labour force but these do not affect any of the conclusions discussed here.

(ii) Young workers and new entrants to the labour force: It is, of course, well known that young workers are much more mobile than their elders, but the size of this group and their relative migration rates are too small to have a significant impact on aggregate labour market adjustment. There are also technical problems in defining migration by those who enter the labour force on completion of their education or training. Is, for example, a 22–year old, whose parents live in the south–east and who has found a job in London but who attended Edinburgh University, to be regarded as a migrant – in labour market terms – or not? Other than differences in aggregate migration rates, patterns of migration for young workers are fairly similar to those for middle–aged workers so that there is no reason to believe that their exclusion biases our conclusions about the relationship between the housing and labour markets.

(iii) Emigrants and workers retiring from the labour force: Again, it is well known that, relative to workers of a similar age, those retiring from the labour force are more likely to migrate. This has one important implication for the process of labour market adjustment which we will discuss below. Apart from this there is no evidence to suggest that the link between migration and retirement affects the process of labour market adjustment. Little is known about the impact of emigration on the labour market. A limited investigation of those considering emigration that we carried out using 1974 data did not suggest that they were much different from other internal migrants.

Subject to these provisos, the main stylised facts which have emerged from our investigations are as follows.

Aggregate migration rates in Britain are low by comparison with those in the United States
There are various difficulties in defining migration on a comparable basis in such geographically different countries as the United Kingdom and the United States. Nonetheless, even on the most stringent measure –

Housing and the National Economy

comparing interregional migration in the United Kingdom with interstate migration in the United States – the United Kingdom has an aggregate migration rate which is only one third of that in the United States (see table 6.1). This gap is narrowed if one adjusts for differences in educational and tenure patterns, but still the United States has migration rates which are over twice British rates.

Table 6.1 Migration and movement rates for the United Kingdom and the United States

(Per cent of heads of households in the labour force)

| | Movement/Migration rates HoH Occupation | | |
	All	Non–manual	Manual
A. UK – *General Household Survey* 1973 – 4			
Movement:All	7.74	9.30	6.57
Job–related	0.99	1.80	0.39
Migration between regions:			
All	1.14	1.83	0.62
Job–related	0.45	0.93	0.10
B. UK – *Labour Force Survey* 1983			
Movement	11.65	12.57	10.62
Migration between regions	1.01	1.35	0.62
C. US – *Panel Survey of Income Dynamics* 1980			
Movement:All	26.03	26.62	25.37
Job–related	3.52	2.68	4.44
Movement across a county line:			
All	6.55	5.96	7.21
Job–related	1.84	1.16	2.60
Migration across a state line:			
All	3.09	2.67	3.56
Job–related	1.16	0.59	1.80

Source: UK – *General Household Surveys* (GHS) 1973, 1974 and *Labour Force Survey* (LFS) 1983.
US – Michigan panel survey of income dynamics family tape 1980.

Note: Movement = relocation to any new address; Migration = relocation to a new region.

Aggregate migration rates in the United Kingdom have been stable with about 1 per cent of heads of household migrating each year throughout the period 1973–86, despite large changes in the overall level of unemployment and in the regional distribution of unemployment. Despite relatively low unemployment there has been net out–migration from the south–east throughout the 1980s and, more generally, there is little evidence of a significant correlation between regional unemployment rates and net in– or out–migration.

For 1973–4 it was possible to divide migrants into those who said that they migrated for 'job–related' reasons and other migrants, while for all of the years examined we have distinguished between 'on–the–job' migrants, that is, migrants who continue to work for the same employer, and 'off–the–job' migrants. The percentage of all migrants who migrated for job–related reasons was just under 40 per cent in Britain, a figure which is quite close to the equivalent percentage in the United States. In Britain the ratio of job–related migrants to all migrants is rather higher for young heads of household (aged under 35) than for older heads of household, whereas the American ratios for these two groups are very similar. Since aggregate migration rates decline more rapidly with age in Britain than in the United States, this implies that job–related migration is much more concentrated among young heads of household in this country. On–the–job migration consistently accounts for nearly 50 per cent of all migration. Much of this migration takes the form of firms transferring workers as a result of promotions and other internal reasons and is thus relatively insensitive to external economic variables. Thus, the amount of 'classical' labour migration which responds to differences in regional labour market conditions is almost negligible in relation to the overall magnitude of unemployment differentials.

Migration patterns for manual workers are quite different from those for non–manual workers
This result may be illustrated by two separate findings. First, the aggregate percentage migration rates by occupational category in 1986 were: professional and managerial, 1.80; junior non–manual, 1.25; personal service workers, 1.34; skilled manual, 0.61; semi– and unskilled manual, 0.60.

In the following discussion we will classify the first two categories – professional and managerial and junior non–manual – as non–manual workers and the rest as manual workers. On this basis the average migration rates over the period 1983–6 were 1.4 per cent for non–manual workers and 0.61 per cent for manual workers. This pattern is quite different from that in the United States, where the migration rate for non–manual workers is about 2.7 per cent as compared with 3.6 per cent for manual workers. The difference between the two countries is even more marked when one looks at job–related migration. In Britain job–related migration accounts for about one half of all non–manual migration but less than 20 per cent of manual migration. On the other hand, in the United States less than one quarter of non–manual migrants moved for job–related reasons whereas over one half of manual migrants moved for job–related reasons. These figures imply that job–related migration is almost exclusively confined to non–manual workers in Britain, whereas in the United States job–related migration is dominated by manual workers.

The second finding concerns the composition of migration flows into and out of different regions. Despite high unemployment rates there was net in–migration of manual workers into the north over 1983–6 and an effective balance between in– and out–migrants for Scotland and Yorkshire–Humberside, and only a very small net out–migration from the West Midlands. On the other hand, for non–manual workers there was substantial out–migration from all of these regions except Scotland. For relatively low unemployment regions, there was much larger net in–migration into the East Midlands for non–manual workers (over 0.6 per cent per annum) than for manual workers (less than 0.3 per cent per annum). Only for East Anglia and Wales was it the case that the net in–migration rate for manual workers exceeded that for non–manual workers. Finally, net out–migration from the south–east was considerably faster for manual workers (0.26 per cent per annum) than for non–manual workers (0.13 per cent per annum). This evidence, and other results discussed below, indicates that non–manual and manual workers respond to labour market imbalances in very different ways

Council tenants are much less likely, ceteris paribus, to migrate or to move house for job – related reasons than are owner – occupiers
For 1973–4 we calculated that migration rates for council tenants were typically less than 20 per cent of those for similar heads of household who were owner–occupiers. In later work we were also able to show that council tenants were no less likely than equivalent owner–occupiers to seek to migrate, so that the much lower realised migration rates were the result of differences in the barriers to migration that they experienced rather than in intentions. The original work has recently been extended to job–related migration. This showed that the difference between job–related migration rates for council tenants and owner–occupiers is smaller than for all migration, but still council tenants experience substantially greater barriers to job–related migration than do owner–occupiers.

The absence of data on tenure one year earlier in most of the Labour Force Surveys makes it difficult to compare the early 1970s and the early 1980s with respect to the impact of tenure on migration. We have been able to carry out some work for 1981 and 1984. This suggests that council tenancy remains a significant barrier to migration but that its importance relative to other factors is less than it was in the earlier period. On the other hand sales of council houses have substantially reduced the proportion of households which are council tenants. This reduction has not been uniform for households with different socio–economic characteristics. Council housing has become much more concentrated among households with heads who are relatively old and are semi– or unskilled manual workers. The general increase in unemployment has tended to increase the existing barriers to migration for these groups, so the lower absolute value of the coefficient on council tenancy may be the result of a general worsening in the migration opportunities for the types of household which tend to concentrate in council housing.

One additional, and very tentative, result is that the negative effect of council tenancy on migration seems to be more severe for unemployed workers. We were not able to examine the interaction between unemployment and tenure with respect to the probability of migration in our original work because of problems of degeneracy due to the (relatively) small sample available. However, for the 1984 Labour Force Survey data, which only provides previous tenure information for households in England and Scotland, we find that the coefficient associated with council tenants who are unemployed is significantly less than zero even when both individual unemployment and council tenancy are included in the model. The explanation for this result almost certainly lies in the role of on-the-job migration. Restrictions on new housebuilding by local authorities during the 1980s had meant that most council tenants who migrate are able to do so only as part of a process of sponsored migration either by their existing employer or as a result of the activities of new town corporations in recruiting labour from other regions. Unemployed workers are not, of course, eligible for on-the-job migration and may not have the skills or other characteristics sought by new town corporations.

The dampening effect of council tenancy on mobility is not confined to migration alone. We have also found that council tenants experience more difficulty in moving locally for job-related reasons than do owner-occupiers even though council tenants have higher rates of local movement for all reasons. The crucial difference is that job-related movement is likely to mean movement beyond the area covered by the council tenant's current landlord, so that some kind of inter-authority house swap or arrangement may be involved. Opportunities for movement between dwellings owned by the same local authority are relatively plentiful and easy to arrange, but a move from one local authority to another is much more difficult, whether this involves migration or not. Thus, council tenants may find that their ability to search neighbouring labour markets for employment opportunities is almost as restricted as their prospects of moving to another region of the country

Unemployment rates are significantly higher, ceteris paribus, for council tenants than for owner–occupiers

Council tenants are more likely, *ceteris paribus*, than owner–occupiers in general to be unemployed. When the category of owner–occupiers is disaggregated, it turns out that the crucial distinction is between owner–occupiers with mortgages and other tenures including those who own the house that they occupy outright. After controlling for other variables, owners with mortgages have unemployment rates which are only 60 per cent of the rates for similar heads of household in other tenure categories. The reason for this seems to be that owner–occupiers with mortgages have a greater incentive to avoid unemployment or, if they become unemployed, to accept an alternative job than do those living in other tenures.

Unemployed workers are more likely, ceteris paribus, to migrate than are those with jobs
There are a number of ways in which migration might contribute to the reduction of regional unemployment differentials. Focussing specifically on labour supply one must examine the separate effects of regional unemployment on unemployed and employed workers. The former are substantially more likely to migrate than are the latter but there is no interaction between the level of regional unemployment and individual unemployment, so that unemployed workers are not more likely to migrate out of high unemployment regions than out of low unemployment regions. Nonetheless, this effect does tend to increase out–migration rates for high unemployment regions since a greater proportion of the population is exposed to the higher migration probability associated with individual unemployment.

When we investigated the impact of unemployment on migration intentions using data for 1974, we found that it was non–manual rather than manual workers who tended to respond to unemployment by seeking to migrate. However, analysis of the data for the 1980s does not indicate any significant interactions between occupation and individual unemployment with respect to the probability of migration.

High levels of regional unemployment tend to discourage out – migration
For both the 1970s and the 1980s we have found that high levels of regional unemployment relative to the national average tends to discourage out–migration, while high vacancy rates tend to encourage out–migration. These results, though they are apparently paradoxical in terms of simple models of labour market adjustment, are not special to Britain. Similar patterns have been observed for both the United States and the Netherlands. The explanation may lie in the nature of the risks facing those currently in employment who may be considering out–migration from a region. A substantial fraction of all migration is temporary in the sense that the migrants move on from their destination region within a period of five years. Much of this subsequent migration takes the form of a return to the region of origin, so that potential migrants must consider the probability that they might find it difficult to obtain another job in their region of origin. On this basis the expected loss associated with an unsuccessful attempt at migration will be higher the higher the level of unemployment in the origin region, which will tend to discourage out–migration by the employed. On the other hand higher vacancy rates reduce the expected loss due to unsuccessful migration and thus work in the opposite direction.

Investigation of the interactions between occupation and regional unemployment and vacancy rates fills out this explanation. The effect of regional unemployment on out–migration is nil for professional and managerial workers. These workers are effectively involved in a national labour market since their unemployment rates are very low with trivial regional differentials. Thus, the risks associated with unsuccessful migration are not determined by local unemployment but by the costs of movement and other considerations. On the other hand, skilled manual workers are more severely affected by local unemployment than are other manual workers. This is presumably a consequence of the specific nature of the manual skills combined with the impact of the structural decline of traditional industries which have been major employers of skilled manual workers. As a consequence skilled manual workers have been either unable or unwilling to migrate, so that structural unemployment has been exacerbated rather than alleviated by migration patterns.

Migrants tend to move from regions with relatively low levels of real wages to regions with higher real wages
This is a straightforward finding in line with standard models of labour market adjustment. It is derived by examining both out–migration decisions and decisions on the choice of destination conditional upon a prior decision to leave the origin region. The coefficient on the real wage is negative in the first equation and positive in the second equation. In some models of migration behaviour, especially those following in the tradition of the Harris–Todaro model for rural–urban migration in developing countries, one would expect to find a positive coefficient on the interaction between the real wage and regional unemployment in the out–migration equation, since higher unemployment reduces the expected value of the real wage, while this interaction would have a negative coefficient in the in–migration equation. We have found that the coefficient on this term in the out–migration equation is indeed positive but it is barely significant, while we have been unable to identify any non–trivial interactions between the real wage and unemployment in the in–migration equation.

There is substantial net HoH manual worker out–migration from the south–east and little net HoH manual worker out–migration from the depressed regions
This is a basic 'perversity' of the United Kingdom labour market in the mid–1980s: while unemployment rates between regions are highly uneven for manual workers, there are net outflows from the largest and most prosperous region. At the same time there is no manual worker net outflow from the four most depressed regions. Thus, the stylised fact that there is, at an aggregate level, net out–migration from the more depressed regions obscures the importance of non–manual workers in generating these net outflows. Tables 6.2 and 6.3 describe gross region out– and in–migration percentage rates using the Labour Force Surveys for 1983–6. Net out–migration from the south–east did not increase between 1983–6 for HoH manual and non–manual workers despite the rise in relative house prices in the south–east. (Net out–migration is found by

101

Table 6.2 Average annual out–migration rates 1983–6 by region and socioeconomic group

Percentage out–migration rates (p.a.)

Region	Manual		Non–manual	
	HoH	Non–HoH	HoH	Non–HoH
South–east	0.766	0.582	1.223	0.923
North–west	0.499	0.668	1.478	0.932
North	0.390	0.407	1.726	1.298
Yorks/Humber	0.541	0.706	2.025	1.621
East Midlands	0.636	0.654	2.068	1.730
East Anglia	0.549	0.768	2.347	1.379
South–west	1.164	0.821	2.060	2.013
West Midlands	0.564	0.540	1.810	1.527
Wales	0.370	0.415	1.881	1.296
Scotland	0.314	0.485	0.906	0.847

Source: Authors' calculations based on *Labour Force Surveys* 1983–6.
Note: The average out–migration rates are calculated as an averge of the percentages of the population living in the region one year earlier who moved out of the region in the periods ending in April/May of 1983–6 when the Labour Force Surveys took place.

Table 6.3 Average annual in–migration rates 1983–6 by region and socioeconomic group

Percentage in–migration rates (p.a.)

Region	Manual		Non–manual	
	HoH	Non–HoH	HoH	Non–HoH
South–east	0.515	0.606	1.096	1.113
North–west	0.532	0.476	1.517	1.121
North	0.568	0.474	1.555	1.140
Yorks/Humber	0.517	0.409	1.779	1.057
East Midlands	0.934	0.765	2.674	2.076
East Anglia	1.095	1.179	2.837	2.717
South–west	1.200	1.233	2.850	2.156
West Midlands	0.504	0.541	1.397	0.853
Wales	0.595	0.622	2.029	1.052
Scotland	0.326	0.443	0.955	0.626

Source: Authors' calculations based on *Labour Force Surveys* 1983–6.
Note: The average in–migration rates are calculated as an average of the percentages of the population living in the region at the time of the surveys who had moved into the region in the year preceding April/May of 1983–6 when the Labour Force Surveys took place.

subtracting the entry in table 6.3 from the relevant entry in table 6.2.) In fact, the most noticeable trend is the rise over this period in gross in–migration rates for both socio–economic groups. Thus, while the south continues to export labour to the rest of the country, there was a tendency for this to be reversed between 1983–6.

House prices do not have a significant effect on in – or out – migration rates other than via their effect on regional real wage levels
House prices are, via their effect on housing costs, the major source of differences in real wages between regions. In our most recent work we used pooled data from the 1983–6 Labour Force Surveys – a sample of about 200,000 heads of households – to examine a variety of models of a two stage process in which individuals first choose whether to leave a region or to stay put and then the migrants among them choose which region to move to. In this framework we have considered numerous ways in which relative regional house prices might affect either of these decisions, either as independent explanatory variables or via their effect on the real wage.

After controlling for the effect of regional differences in real wages and other variables, our results indicate that higher house prices have only a slight effect on *out – migration* levels and this is concentrated among those workers aged over 54 who migrate without changing their employer. It appears that such workers are encouraged to move from regions with high house prices to those with lower house prices. Presumably any financial contribution from their employers towards their moving costs enhances the attraction of such a move by reducing the costs involved in realising a proportion of the capital which they have accumulated in the form of housing equity and in reducing future expenditures on housing. On the other hand, real wage levels in a region do not appear to exercise a significant influence on out–migration so that a change in house prices does not affect out–migration via its impact on real wages.

Turning to the choice of destination we may ask whether migrants avoid regions with high house prices. Again, we find no independent effect for house prices when real wages and other variables are included in the model, except that migrants aged over 54 are mildly deterred by high house prices. Lower average real wages in a region do have the effect of reducing in–migration to the region, so that increased house prices operate via their impact on real wages.

When we add together the various effects of a 10 per cent rise in a region's house prices relative to those elsewhere, the impact on total out–migration rates is negligible (see table 6.4) while the change in the distribution of destination choices is quite small (see table 6.5). This is partly because the old have low migration rates, so that very large changes in their migration behaviour are required if there is to be significant impact on total migration flows. We estimate that a 10 per cent rise in relative house prices in the south–east will reduce net in–migration by less than 1,000 households per year; only a small fraction of this reduction will be comprised of manual workers. This suggests that annual fluctuations in migration are highly unlikely to have a noticeable effect on the determination of wages for over three million manual workers in the south–east.

There is an important further point which should be noted. As mentioned above, our investigations have focussed on migration by members of the labour force. However, it is well known that retiring members of the labour force tend to move out of the south–east to other regions of the country with lower house prices. Our results show that this process operates for those nearing retirement as well as those who have already retired. In effect, high house prices in the south–east may serve as a form of pension capital which can be realised as households approach retirement. Indeed, it is possible that the greater the value of this capital (that is, the greater the house price differentials between the south–east and the rest of the country), the earlier will such households tend to retire. It follows that high house prices in the south–east may

Table 6.4 Predicted out–migration rates under alternative assumptions

| | Migration rates per 1,000 heads of household | | | |
| | 1986 actual values | 10% higher unemployment rates | 10% larger wage differ–entials | 10% larger house price differentials |
	1	2	3	4
All HoHs	11.0	10.5	11.0	11.0
Employed HoHs	10.1	9.6	10.1	10.1
Unemployed HoHs	20.3	19.1	20.3	20.3
Age group (years)				
<35	19.9	18.9	20.0	19.9
35–54	8.2	7.9	8.2	8.3
55+	3.3	3.1	3.3	3.5
Occupational group				
Professional/ managerial	18.0	17.8	18.0	18.0
Junior non–manual	13.2	12.5	13.2	13.1
Personal service	13.8	13.4	13.8	14.0
Skilled manual	6.1	5.6	6.2	6.2
Semi/unskilled manual	6.0	5.1	6.0	6.1

Source: Authors' calculations.

enhance labour market flexibility by facilitating the replacement of older workers by younger workers with different skills. For this reason it would be misleading to use data on population flows between regions to gauge the consequences of migration for the size and nature of the working population.

Table 6.5 Predicted distribution of migration destination choices

Region	% distribution of destination choices for:		
	1986 actual values	10% larger wage differentials	10% larger house price differentials
	1	3	4
North	4.8	4.8	4.9
Yorks/Humber	9.0	8.8	9.0
East Midlands	11.9	11.7	12.0
East Anglia	6.6	6.7	6.6
South–east	26.4	27.1	26.2
South–west	12.3	12.2	12.3
West Midlands	8.4	8.3	8.4
North–west	10.2	10.1	10.2
Wales	5.2	5.1	5.2
Scotland	5.2	5.2	5.2

Source: Authors' calculations.

Aggregate migration flows do not tend to reduce regional unemployment differentials
As noted above, the overall impact of regional unemployment on the pattern of migration flows depends on the separate effects of unemployment on the unemployed and on the employed which operate in different directions. Simulation of the full set of out– and in–migration equations shows that it is the effect of regional unemployment on the employed which dominates, so that an increase in regional unemployment differentials tends to reduce overall migration and to lessen the level of out–migration from regions with high unemployment. Thus, our results suggest that migration has contributed little to reducing existing differentials in regional unemployment rates. Note, again, that this conclusion is much stronger for manual workers – especially skilled manual workers – because of their low overall migration rates and the dampening effect of unemployment on the migration behaviour of employed manual workers.

Housing policy and labour market performance
Four major targets for the reform of housing policies have been proposed so as to enhance the performance of the labour market. These are first, the organisation of the council housing system; second, rent controls in the private rental sector; third, tax concessions for owner–occupiers, and fourth, the system of land–use planning. Any discussion of the relative importance of policies in each of these areas must be on a view as to what are the major distortions in the labour market that have been influenced by housing policies.

Regional variations in unemployment rates for manual workers – the popular basis for arguments about the north–south divide – seem to be the best indicator of the welfare losses that housing policies may generate or aggravate. The relatively low rates of interregional migration for United Kingdom manual workers suggest that this market suffers from a failure to match workers and job openings efficiently, which results in a loss of output and underutilisation of resources in the economy as a whole. The evidence suggests that housing policies may be important contributory factors leading to market failure in the manual labour market. In contrast, the relatively even unemployment rates for non–manual workers across regions and their high rates of interregional mobility prompt the conclusion that the non–manual labour market can be regarded as an integrated national market. There is little evidence in this case that housing policies have caused efficiency losses on a similar scale to those in the market for manual labour.

Bover, Muellbauer and Murphy (1988) would maintain that the welfare losses which arise from the *extra* volatility of relative regional house prices that results from the fiscal bias in favour of owner–occupied housing is also very important. The empirical effect of the tax treatment of owner–occupation on the *volatility* of relative regional house prices is unclear, though, of course, such policies have raised the general *level* of house prices across the country as a whole. We are, therefore, not persuaded on *a priori* grounds that the welfare losses in the labour market due to the tax treatment of owner–occupied housing are large relative to the magnitude of the losses described above in the manual labour market which are strongly influenced by distortions affecting the rented housing sector. There is a strong case for reforming the taxation of owner–occupied housing, but on current evidence we are sceptical about arguments for reform based on labour market considerations.

The primary objective in attempting to bring housing and labour market policies together should be to mitigate the separation of local labour markets for manual workers in order to eliminate the disparities which persist in the employment opportunities available to workers in different parts of the country. How is this to be done? Reform in the council housing sector is crucial since 27 per cent of all households and a majority of those with manual heads remain in this sector. It is not good enough for economists to write council housing off or to suggest that reform is politically difficult or unlikely to succeed. There is substantial housing mobility within the local authority rented sector for non–job–related reasons; what is required is a determined effort to manage council housing in a manner that facilitates job–related mobility for manual workers. Simple policies of privatisation or yet more subsidies to those who purchase their council houses will have the reverse effect because they will tend to strengthen rather than weaken the link between a household's location and access to or the level of housing subsidies.

In the short term the Department of the Environment could improve matters within the current system by requiring that each local authority should reserve a larger fraction of its council house relets for those moving into the district from another part of the country. An increase in the proportion of relets allocated in this way from 1–5 per cent might be appropriate in the light of the experience of the National Mobility Scheme. A relatively simple administrative change along these lines could have a significant immediate impact on the flow of manual workers between regions. The primary beneficiaries would be younger skilled manual workers who would like to move to the more prosperous and lower unemployment regions of the country. Such a scheme could be targeted specifically at the unemployed, in which case it should also be combined with the provision of appropriate forms of job training, but such targeting might simply increase the administrative costs of the scheme without contributing to its overall impact on local labour markets.

This proposal would exacerbate existing imbalances between the demand for and supply of council housing in different parts of the country, with some families in the south now being displaced from the council sectorl. A strong case may be made for reforming the present arrangements governing the finance, construction and management of public housing. These have resulted in a relative under–provision of local authority housing in the more prosperous and usually Conservative–controlled local authorities as well as a concentration of highly subsidised but often poorly managed council housing in the metropolitan areas. The reallocation of capital resources for the new construction of subsidised rental housing from local authorities to the Housing Corporation and thus housing associations should improve the situation slowly, since housing associations tend to be more responsive to market factors in deciding upon the volume and character of their new building. Even so, local authority control over planning matters and the limited administrative capacity of many housing associations may require central intervention either by the Department of the Environment or by the Housing Corporation to ensure that more attention is paid in future to local labour market conditions when finance is allocated for the construction of new subsidised housing.

Unfortunately, current policies for the reform of local authority housing may – at least during the transitional period – further reduce regional mobility for council tenants. 'Privatisation' of the council housing stock is likely to result in patchwork of small landlords – either private or voluntary housing associations – administering public housing at controlled rents so long as existing tenants continue to occupy their dwellings. New tenants will be expected to pay rents which are much nearer to market levels, so that there is little incentive for tenants in depressed areas to move to more prosperous areas of the country since the expected income gain would have to be sufficient to compensate for the loss of their previous rent subsidy. Equally, there will be no reason for landlords to enter exchange schemes which enable tenants to move from less prosperous areas to tenancies at controlled rents in high employment areas. Despite the other potential benefits of these reforms it is clear that their implications for labour mobility have been underestimated. This is not an argument for either reversing or slowing down the process of change since the problems lie in the awkward combinations of subsidy and market forces that are likely to result from the privatisation of council housing. What is needed now is to ensure that the transition to market–determined rents and subsidies which are tied to household circumstances rather than houses takes place rapidly and should not be delayed by uncertainty or confusion about the direction and objectives of the reforms.

After the conference in December 1988, from which this book arises, the government announced its intention to introduce further changes to the current system of local authority housing finance under a new Local Government and Housing Bill to come into effect in April 1990. One aspect of these changes – the restriction of new local authority housebuilding to the provision of special purpose dwellings for the elderly or similar groups – is simply a formal recognition of the *de facto* outcome of current policies. The more radical aspect of the new arrangements is the decision to bring council rents into line with notional market rents based on the current capital values of dwellings instead of the current system of rent pooling. The details and timing of the consequent increases in rents remain to be settled but the intention is clear. The government wishes to encourage migration from the south–east to the rest of the country by ensuring that relative rent levels in different parts of the country reflect both local house prices and the balance between the demand for and supply of council accomodation in different localities. It expects that council rents in London and the south–east may be increased to double or triple their present level in real terms over a transitional period of five to ten years and it believes that this will provide the appropriate signal to encourage both workers and firms to move away from areas with high house prices. At the same time the changes will encourage better management of the stock of council houses and a higher rate of utilisation in aggregate.

The real level of council rents has increased substantially during the 1980s because of the financial restrictions imposed on local authorities and there are already significant differentials between rents in London and in the depressed regions, so the new policy will be more an extension of existing trends rather than a radical departure from past patterns. Further, the practical significance of changes in rent levels should not be overstated. Over one half of council tenants in London and other metropolitan areas receive housing benefit; this proportion has been growing along with the average age of council tenants and with the percentage of council tenants who are retired. Higher rents will mean that many more council tenants will become eligible for housing benefit so that their overall impact will depend upon any accompanying adjustments to the housing benefit scales.

Suppose that we accept that the new policy will result in large increases in council rents in London and the south–east. Will it then achieve the government's objective of encouraging migration from these areas to the rest of the country? In terms of the empirical work discussed above, doubling rents in London would have the effect of reducing real wages for council tenants in London relative to those in the rest of the country by between 10 and 20 per cent. Drawing on the figures in tables 6.2–6.5 we calculate that this might increase the average out–migration rate for manual workers from 7.6 to 7.9 per 1,000 HoHs while the in–migration rate might fall from 5.2 to 4.9 per 1,000 HoHs. The net level of out–migration for manual workers would thus increase from 2.4 to 3.0 per 1,000 HoHs and even this figure assumes that the usual barriers facing council tenants who wish to migrate have been reduced at the same time as rents are increased. In aggregate terms this shift is equivalent to an extra 3,000 manual households a year moving out of London and the south–east to other parts of the country. This is an order of magnitude smaller than the figure of 300,000 households moving over a period of five to ten years to fill vacant council housing outside the south–east which was the target announced by the Secretary of State when he introduced the new policy.

There are many arguments which need to be considered in assessing the overall merits of these proposals for local authority housing finance and rents. However, we can assert with confidence that our investigations offer no empirical support for the view that higher council rents will, on their own, encourage a substantial new outflow of migrants from the south–east. Administrative changes in methods of allocating council tenancies are likely to be much more important in determining the migration behaviour of current or potential council tenants. Finally, a reduction in regional differentials in unemployment rates would have much more impact on the migration patterns for manual workers than will any plausible adjustments in council rents.

Comment on Chapter 6

Alan W Evans

In this chapter Hughes and McCormick summarise the results of their research over the last few years on the relationship between mobility, migration and housing tenure and comment on the implications of their research for the reform of 'the organisation of the council house system'. Their view is that the present council house system impedes migration by tenants and so reduces the efficiency of the labour market. Thus growing firms in areas of low unemployment suffer from labour shortages, whilst unemployed workers elsewhere are restrained from moving because that would mean giving up existing tenancies. So economic growth is lower than it would be and unemployment higher than it should be.

Their proposals regarding the allocation of a proportion of relets to migrants and the construction of more local authority housing in the more prosperous parts of the country have some merit but are unlikely to be implemented. A major reason is that little local authority housing is now being constructed. The number of dwellings completed has fallen consistently from about 130,000 in 1976 to less than 20,000 in 1987 and is planned to fall further. Moreover the stock of local authority dwellings has been reduced as they have been sold to their occupiers. More recently many Conservative controlled areas have begun to take advantage of recent legislation to try to divest themselves of what remains.

There is no reason to suppose that this trend will be reversed. Maybe Hughes and McCormick can congratulate themselves that their observations on the inefficiency of the council housing sector have borne fruit in terms of policy, even if not the fruit they intended, but I suspect that the decline of council housing results from a coupling of political interest with ideology. Ideologically, the view of the present government is that wherever possible the size of the public sector should be reduced, and that owner occupation is *per se* a good thing. Politically, it is widely perceived, both on the left and right, that council tenants tend to vote Labour and owner–occupiers are more likely to vote Conservative (or SLD or SDP). A reduction in the size of the local authority sector is therefore to the long–term political disadvantage of the Labour party.

Nevertheless the reduction in the size of the sector, for whatever reason, does improve mobility and thus a method for enhancing labour market performance and so achieving Hughes and McCormick's objectives. Moreover the empirical work by Muellbauer and Murphy (1988a), reported in Chapter 4, confirm that an increase in potential mobility appears to be positively correlated with an increase in migration into the south–east.

Housing and land supply

The shift from local authority housing so that new housing construction is almost wholly left to the private sector is not neutral so far as the housing and land markets are concerned. In this book the implications of the land use planning system have been almost entirely neglected, possibly because very few economists have any understanding of the topic. In my view this neglect is mistaken. The British town and country planning system is a major cause of the slow economic growth of the British economy (Evans, 1988; Cheshire *et al.*, 1985) and interacts with the labour market because of the way it limits the supply of land.

That the supply is restricted has been a matter of argument (Grigson, 1986; Evans, 1987) but, in my view, is made obvious by comparing the price of agricultural land in the south–east – £5,000 per hectare in October 1987 (Property Market Review) – with the price of land with permission for residential development – £1 million per hectare at that date outside Greater London. It follows that because the supply of land is severely restricted the price of housing is high, particularly in the south–east, when the level of demand is high (which is not to say, that the supply of land is not as important as demand in determining price levels).

In this context the reduction in the size of the local authority sector is likely to affect the market for housing in the private sector in ways which are little appreciated.

Firstly, many local authority tenants are likely to occupy smaller dwellings than they would choose in the private sector. A study by Olsen (1972) demonstrated that this appeared to be true for tenants of rent controlled properties in New York City. Given a choice between a smaller low cost unit and a larger higher cost unit, many chose the former. Thus many local authority flat dwellers would not freely choose to live in a flat but do so because it is offered to them and it is cheap. Of course many tenants may actually occupy larger dwellings than they would wish to own or rent in a free market. Nevertheless it would seem that those who are likely to be motivated to buy and then move are those who occupy less space than they would wish. Those who occupy more space than they would wish are less likely to wish to move.

House sales which encourage mobility serve to increase the demand for housing as households which have exercised the right to buy attempt to move on to better accommodation. If private sector housing supply is limited this serves to drive up house prices. Secondly, the provision of housing in the public sector is supply led whilst its provision in the private sector is necessarily demand led, and the shift from one to the other has important consequences for the land market. Suppose a local authority decides that a certain number of council houses are needed. It can go out to buy the land needed. If necessary it can use its powers of compulsory purchase; it is also more likely to give itself planning permission for development. Thus land can be bought at the current market price, and the houses built and occupied. But for the private sector to provide the houses it has to buy the land and/or obtain planning permission. The price of land, and the price of houses, have to rise to a level at which landowners will willingly sell the land for development, and this must be above the current market price for at that price they would not willingly sell.

Clearly the price of land must be higher than if it was compulsory purchased, for otherwise powers of compulsory purchase would not be necessary. (A demonstration of the reasons why landowners may not willingly sell land to developers at the current market price can be found in papers by Evans, 1983; Neutze, 1987; and Wiltshaw 1988). Furthermore local authorities may be less willing to give planning permission to ('greedy') developers for (speculative) housing than they would be to themselves for ('socially beneficial') housing.

The combined effect of the diversion of housing from the public sector to the private sector is to add a further impetus to the spiralling land and house prices of the mid–1980s. Some empirical evidence for this view is the negative correlation between house prices and local authority house construction in Mayes' (1979) econometric model of the housing market.

House prices and migration

The fact that increased demand for housing tends to lead to higher house prices because of supply restrictions is very relevant to the work of Hughes and McCormick. They assume that increased mobility is beneficial and will lead to higher economic growth. Implicitly they assume that increased demand will bring forth an increased housing supply. Recent work by Rosen and Topel (1988) suggests that in the United States the elasticity of supply is high even in the short run and very high indeed in the long run. Everything points to the fact that the elasticity of supply in the United Kingdom is very low indeed so that increases in demand result merely in increases in price. And of course these increases in price serve to choke off migration as work by Muellbauer and Murphy tends to confirm.

So if one constraint on labour mobility is eased another takes its place, and one with considerable political backing, for the land use planning system in the south-east is operated to support the status quo and build as few houses as possible for migrants from elsewhere. (Only recently north-east Hampshire just outside the London green belt with almost the lowest unemployment rate in the country, was planning for net out-migration in the 1990s!).

The political backing for the system is high because of the paradoxes of a system of owner occupation. As house prices rise because of increased demand, existing owner occupiers feel better off, the more so if wages rise because of labour shortages. Thus real wages may be high for existing residents. At the same time immigrants may find that the higher wages do not fully compensate them for the higher house prices that they have to pay. The situation would be different if properties were tenanted, since increased demand would raise rents and tenants would then be more willing for the supply of housing to be increased. But as things are at present there is little pressure on existing residents to support any increase in housing supply. Residents adjacent to possible green field sites will resist development and there will be political advantages in arguing that development should go elsewhere. Thus restriction on mobility in the form of council house tenancies is replaced by a house price differential which serves the same purpose.

7 The viability of the privately rented housing market

Christine Whitehead and Mark Kleinman

Introduction

The Housing Act 1988 puts into place a legal framework for new lettings within the privately rented housing sector which in principle allows the market to operate freely. Two types of contract will be possible: (a) assured tenancies, where tenants have the right to continuing security of tenure as long as they meet their contractual obligations and are prepared to pay the market rent; and (b) assured/shorthold tenancies where security is limited to a fixed term. In addition the reasons for eviction have been extended so that landlords will generally be able to gain possession whenever contractual conditions are consistently broken.

Rents are to be freely agreed between landlord and tenant. In principle one would therefore expect rents to vary inversely with the extent of security offered: greater security should mean higher rents, reflecting the landlords' loss of flexibility. Again, in principle tenants should be able to choose the range of conditions and related prices which best meet their preferences. Thus in the longer term the sector will be made up of willing landlords providing accommodation to tenants prepared to pay the market price (see Department of the Environment, 1987a, b and c).

In these conditions as long as there are some potential landlords

We are grateful for financial assistance from the Nuffield Foundation and Joseph Rowntree Memorial Trust and to the London Research Centre and the Halifax Building Society for access to data.

113

and some tenants who wish to be in the market there will be a viable sector. But what size that sector will be and which households will be accommodated there depend upon the range of housing and other options available to both potential landlords and potential tenants. Freeing up the regulatory framework is thus only one element in the equation.

The objective of deregulation is to bring about a structural change in the operation of the housing market. It is therefore difficult to assess what may happen simply by examining how the market has worked in the past. It is however possible to suggest what are likely to be the main determinants of change. In this chapter we discuss some of the factors which will affect the likely size and composition of the rented sector. To do this we look first at the current position in the sector. We then examine the characteristics of potential tenants and the rents and rates of return likely to be required by potential landlords. Finally we bring these elements together to assess the overall viability of the sector within the current housing system.

Current position

The private rented sector currently houses less than 8 per cent of households in Britain. It has been declining throughout most of the century and the rate of decline has not slowed down as the sector has become smaller. The number of households renting privately has fallen by nearly one half during the 1970s and perhaps by a further third since 1981[1] (Department of the Environment, 1988a).

Despite its small size, the sector is very heterogeneous in terms of the types of households that are found there. Broadly speaking we can distinguish four main categories: first, households whose accommodation is related to their employment; secondly, the rump of the traditional private rented sector; thirdly, a near market sector catering for young, mobile and newly-forming households; and fourthly, a residual element reflecting the sector's role as 'tenure of last resort'.

According to the 1981 Census there were 374,000 households in the first category, representing about 2 per cent of households overall and some 19 per cent of private tenants (OPCS, 1983). By definition, this category provides housing for those in particular occupations – mainly agricultural workers and members of the armed services, but also caretakers, police, some hospital workers, and so on. The incentives both to supply and to live in such accommodation relate to the perceived need for the employee to be readily available in a particular location. Provision is thus based more on the attributes of the labour market than on the housing market. The rent is rarely related to the cost of provision but is rather reflected in lower wage rates. This sub-sector has been declining at least at an equivalent rate to that of the sector as a whole, in part as a result of employment decline in the relevant sectors, in part because of changes in attitude away from such provision by both landlords and tenants. There has been no sign of any revival of this sub-sector, even in areas of particular difficulty in finding rented accommodation.

The second category is still the largest of the four elements, and comprises all those households who have traditionally lived in the sector. Most of these households are poor, and very many are elderly. They have usually been private tenants all their lives, often in the same dwelling. Typically, they occupy whole houses (not flats or multi–occupied property), and rent unfurnished on regulated ('fair') rents which are usually below market levels. Dwellings are likely to be in poor repair, unmodernised and perhaps lacking amenities. In 1981 over one third of all households lacking either bath or WC were in the unfurnished sector where the group is concentrated. Unfitness (18 per cent of private rented dwellings in England as compared to 5 per cent of owner–occupied and 1 per cent of public sector dwellings in 1981) and disrepair (42 per cent as compared to 21 per cent in the owner–occupied sector and 12 per cent in the public sector) are also concentrated among this group (Whitehead and Kleinman, 1986). Since then, while the absolute number of households affected has declined, the concentration of problems has remained (Department of the Environment, 1988b).

The incentives and constraints in the traditional sector are fairly well–defined. Rent control and security of tenure have made it possible and, in comparison to alternatives, desirable for these, mainly poor, households already housed in the sector to remain there. Regulation has also stopped landlords from leaving until their dwellings become vacant but has given them little or no incentive to repair and improve these dwellings. While some units have undoubtedly been relet on vacancy, in so doing most have been transferred to less regulated parts of the sector and the majority of vacancies have been sold into owner–occupation. Hence, this part of the private rented sector is a legacy from the time when private renting was the norm, a stratum which has been preserved from the tenure transformation of the intervening decades through the twin mechanism of rent control (which has kept properties affordable by poor households) and security of tenure (which has prevented landlords from selling the property for owner–occupation).

As a result of the Housing Act there will no longer be new fair rent lettings, so this part of the private rented sector will disappear over the next decades as households die, dissolve or move into other tenures. Any overall revival in private renting must therefore involve inducing enough new lettings to offset this automatic decline.

The third category is very different, and possesses some of the characteristics of a market sector. It includes (among others) newly–forming households (single people, couples and larger multi–adult groups), younger, employed (mainly non–manual) households who need to move frequently for career reasons, owner–occupiers who require temporary accommodation between the sale of one property and the purchase of another, students, and recently divorced or separated people who need short–term accommodation.

Households in the third category mainly require short or medium–term rather than long–term accommodation. In many cases they are 'en route' to owner–occupation. The types of dwellings they rent include flats, bedsits, and multi–occupied properties as well as single unit houses. Lettings are usually furnished, and rents set by agreement rather than by the rent officer. Rent levels are thus much closer to market rents and generally higher than elsewhere in the sector. In London, for instance, evidence from the GLC Private Rented Sector Survey in 1983/4 suggested that these near–market rents were often as much as three times the equivalent fair rent (Greater London Council, 1986). In Sheffield, another area where detailed surveys have been carried out in the last few years, the ratios appear to be fairly similar (see Crook and Martin, 1988).

Because these tenants are volunteers, they have generally positive reasons for being in the sector. In the main these relate to the easy access nature of the accommodation and the relatively low transactions costs of moving. Landlords similarly have a choice about whether or not to provide. Many who do so are individuals who have purchased property from the regulated sector and relet in the less regulated furnished market. The evidence from Crook and Martin suggests that landlords in Sheffield had still, in so doing, been able to increase rents by nearly ten times between 1979 and 1985 although at the same time their costs of letting had gone up. More general evidence (for example, Todd, 1988) suggests that a high proportion of lettings were acquired during the 1980s, and indeed that many landlords were fairly new to letting.

The final category consists of households who are forced into the private rented sector because they are unable to gain access to other tenures. The group includes those unable to obtain, or still awaiting social sector housing, as well as a small number of those evicted from the social sector or declared 'intentionally homeless' or who have had their owner–occupied dwellings repossessed. This part of the private rented sector shades off almost imperceptibly into what we have elsewhere called 'non–tenure' accommodation – hostels, bed and breakfast accommodation, squats and short–life property (Whitehead and Kleinman, 1986). Almost by definition these tenants have little capacity to pay for adequate accommodation, and are dependent on housing benefit, which is available to almost everyone who is able to find somewhere to live. For this sub–sector to survive, landlords must be willing to let to such tenants – for in the main this sub–sector is subject to rapid turnover so landlords are able to escape if they wish. Indeed there is at least anecdotal evidence that certain landlords prefer DSS tenants because the rent is more likely to be forthcoming. Certainly, at the margin, these tenants compete with those in the third category who are choosing to rent privately.

Thus the major dynamics within the private rented sector at present consist of overall decline with a relative shift from the traditional long–term secure unfurnished sector to the more flexible, easier access sector consisting mainly of furnished units. Even so this more freely working sector still accounts for less than 40 per cent of all lettings. The process involves a spatial shift towards London, where at least one third of all furnished lettings are located, and a change in the style of landlord, mainly towards non–resident individuals and away from companies and those with larger holdings who traditionally took a longer view of their investments. Within this sector, there are two distinct types of households – those who wish and can afford to be in the private rented sector and those who are there in default of more suitable accommodation and who are generally dependent upon government assistance to pay the rent (Whitehead and Kleinman, 1986).

Table 7.1 Household characteristics of private tenants, Great Britain, 1985 (percentages)

	Unfurnished	Furnished
Age of head of household		
Under 30	12	62
30–64	35	32
65 and over	52	6
Household type		
One adult under 60	12	48
Two adults under 60	9	22
Small family	11	7
Large family	3	0
Large adult household	7	15
Pensioner couple	22	2
Single pensioner	36	5
Socio – economic group of head		
Professionals	1	9
Employers/managers	6	12
Other non–manual	11	36
Skilled manual	11	15
Semi–skilled	8	11
Unskilled	2	2
Economically inactive	62	14
Household income		
Median income as % of all households (economically active only)	72.5	79.4

Source: *General Household Survey* 1985 (OPCS, 1987).

Which groups are likely to demand privately rented housing?
The best evidence we have about who are likely to be the tenants in any future private rented sector is that relating to recent movers, because the vast majority of such lettings are perceived by both landlord and

tenant to be outside the Rent Acts (Todd and Foxan, 1987). Evidence on the furnished sub–sector is also useful because the distinction between furnished and unfurnished very roughly approximates to the distinction between market and regulated sectors (Bovaird *et al.*, 1985). Evidence on London is particularly relevant because private renting in the capital houses a wider range of tenants and plays a larger role in the housing system than in the rest of the country (Whitehead and Kleinman, 1987).

Table 7.1 shows some household characteristics of those in the furnished sector in Britain as compared to those in the unfurnished. Households coming into private renting are clearly very different from those traditionally in the sector, being mainly young, single or childless couples, and notably in non–manual occupations. Even so, their incomes, although higher than those in the unfurnished sector, are still

Table 7.2 Household characteristics: 1984 (percentages)

	All private tenants England	London	Recent movers England	London
Age of head				
Under 31	27.2	37.0	61.9	72.3
31–60	38.5	35.5	33.3	25.7
61 and over	34.4	27.5	4.8	1.9
Household type				
Single adult	16.8	24.4	32.5	36.9
Two adults	17.1	21.3	29.2	32.0
Small family	14.3	9.8	16.9	9.2
Large family	4.7	3.0	4.2	1.5
Large adult household	13.6	15.9	12.5	17.5
Older adult	13.5	8.2	1.7	2.4
Single pensioner	19.9	17.5	3.0	0.5
Socio – economic group of head				
Professionals	4.0	5.9	6.7	9.3
Employer/managers	8.7	9.9	8.1	10.4
Other non–manual	11.3	19.0	16.3	19.7
Skilled	9.9	8.8	8.4	6.2
Semi–skilled	10.4	8.1	10.2	11.4
Unskilled	2.2	2.2	2.1	2.6
Economically inactive	48.4	41.9	38.0	35.2
% job related lettings	17.5	15.4	11.9	10.2

Source: Department of Employment, unpublished data from the *Labour Force Survey* 1984.

less than 80 per cent of the all-household figure.

Table 7.2 provides comparable information for recent movers as compared with more established tenants for England and for London separately. Again it shows the predominance of one- or two-person young adult households in non-manual occupations. A similar picture was found in the OPCS survey of recent lettings carried out between 1982 and 1984 (Todd and Foxan, 1987). In this survey, 70 per cent of recent furnished lettings, and 43 per cent of recent unfurnished lettings, went to households aged under 30. In terms of social class (which differs from

Table 7.3 Recent movers and established private tenants in London, 1986 (percentages)

	Recent movers	Established tenants
Age of head		
Under 31	75	25
31–64	25	41
65 and over	–	34
Household type		
Pensioner only	1	35
Single people	31	17
Two or more adults	54	28
One parent family	0	2
Small family	11	15
Large family	2	3
Economic status of head		
Working full-time	64	49
Working part-time	3	4
Retired	0	31
Unemployed	12	6
Sick/disabled	1	1
Student	18	4
Housewife	2	5
Household income		
Under £5,200	26	45
£5,200–10,400	31	26
£10,400–20,800	25	26
Over £20,800	20	7

Source: London Planning Advisory Committee, 1988 and London Research Centre, 1988.

Socio–Economic Group (SEG) in assigning every household to a class whether economically active or not), 51 per cent of recent lettings went to households in the non–manual social classes.

More up–to–date and detailed information on the characteristics of those moving into the sector is available for London, based on the 1986 London Housing Survey (London Research Centre, 1988). Table 7.3 compares the attributes of recent movers and established tenants. Again, the profile of recent movers is very different from that of established tenants. In particular it suggests that the role of the sector in London has already become mainly that of housing the mobile employed. More than half of new tenant households consisted of two or more adults without children, with a further 31 per cent being single people. Three fourths of new entrants were aged under 31, and none were over pensionable age.

Nearly two thirds of new tenants worked full–time, compared with less than half of established tenants. A further 18 per cent were students. Average incomes of households entering the sector in London were £12,000, as against £6,000 in the council sector, and £7,000 in the Housing Association sector. One fifth of new private tenants had household incomes of over £21,000, compared with only 7 per cent of established tenants. These high household incomes can however, to a considerable degree, be explained by the very large proportion of multi–adult, and thus multi–earning, households rather than as a product of high individual incomes.

The evidence from the 1986/7 survey as well as more general evidence of the growth of homelessness among both families and young people suggests (Audit Commission, 1989), not surprisingly, that the economically active are able to outbid those outside the labour market. This is reflected in the relatively low level of benefit claimants among recent movers – 30 per cent receiving one or another form of benefit and only 20 per cent receiving housing benefit. For all this 12 per cent of new tenants were unemployed compared with only 6 per cent of established tenants – so the sector still to some degree fulfils the role of tenure of last resort, as well as that for the mobile work seeker.

Perhaps the most important attribute of London private renting however was its very rapid turnover rate. In 1986/7 38 per cent of tenants had moved into their accommodation in the last year – compared with only 20 per cent three years earlier. This reflects both the continuing rapid decline of the traditional sector and higher mobility among recent entrants.

While recent movers differ significantly from longer–term tenants the types of dwelling in which they live are very similar, with over 40 per cent in each category obtaining houses rather than flats or rooms. The proportion living in rooms (13 per cent) appears to have fallen rapidly in the last few years, implying that the general quality of accommodation is rising with fewer bedsits and more shared houses. Again this reflects a rather more up–market sector than in the past and suggests that in many ways the accommodation obtained is similar to that available to young first–time buyers.

Thus, in London the private rented sector is already being transformed from its traditional role of providing long–term secure accommodation for families and pensioners at below–market rents, to a more market–orientated role of providing short or medium–term housing for younger, employed and student households. This process is more advanced in London than elsewhere. At the same time, while its role as a tenure of last resort for non–family households remains, that role has become less important and shades into a range of non–tenured accommodation on the margin of the housing system.

It is difficult to obtain comparable evidence from other areas of the country. What we do know is that homelessness and non–tenure accommodation is heavily concentrated in London (Audit Commission, 1989, Conway and Kemp, 1985). One would therefore expect to find that outside London the private rented sector was able to house significant numbers of those at the bottom end of the system, particularly non–labour force participants. Second, the demand for short– and medium–term accommodation for employed workers is likely to be less outside the capital, because of London's position at the apex of the national hierarchy. Third, access to owner–occupation is easier outside the south–east because prices vary more across regions than incomes so fewer employed people might be expected to rent privately. Evidence from Sheffield bears this out to a significant degree. In the 1985 survey Crook and Martin (1988) found that most new lettings were made to those under 30 years old, and that two thirds of all new lettings were to students or the unemployed. In the furnished sector this proportion rose to 78 per cent. So few of those who could afford owner–occupation chose to rent. In the unfurnished market however over half of new tenants were in manual occupations and a quarter had children below school–leaving age, suggesting that in Sheffield there is still a continuing, if limited, role for the traditional private rented sector. Even here 27 per cent of new tenants were unemployed. Sheffield therefore suggests that in areas of general balance in the housing market, private renting plays a very specialist and mainly residual role with only a small easy access market for employed households.

Clearly the future will not be simply an extension of the past because opportunities and constraints will be modified (Kemp, 1988b, Kleinman and Whitehead, 1988). From the point of view of tenants the main areas of possible changes are as follows. First, income: at what rate will it grow for those in work, and how generous will the housing benefit system be for those at the bottom of the scale? Second, the price and availability of housing in other tenures: here the relevant issues are the extent of decline in access to the social sector and the relative benefits of owner–occupation. Third, changes in taste: will preferences shift away from owner–occupation towards renting? The best guess is that it will probably take many years to modify peoples' attitudes to private renting, however desirable the accommodation provided. Fourth, the numbers of potential tenants: the size of the cohort of 18 year–olds is now beginning to decline, even though the number of households is expected to continue to grow well into the next century. Fifth, the price tenants have to pay for private renting: this depends mainly upon landlords' preparedness to provide a range of accommodation at rents which make renting privately a desirable choice.

Landlords' required returns

Landlords have many reasons for being in the private rented sector, including for instance: helping out friends, relatives or employees; property inheritance, and getting some help with the mortgage, as well as strictly commercial reasons. Even within the 'commercial' sector landlords may be looking for quite different attributes: continuing rental returns, lower returns but the capacity to regain vacant possession, capital gains or perhaps simply a relatively easy life. Reasons for letting vary between landlord type and size of holding in a fairly consistent fashion. Many resident landlords want help with the mortgage rather than a commercial return. Among non–resident landlords, companies and institutions are more likely to be looking for an adequate rental return on market value, individuals with smaller holdings are interested in returns on investment but are more likely to stress freedom to realise capital values, while individuals letting single units often

Table 7.4 Recent lettings

(a) 1983 – 4 *by landlord type* (*percentages*)(N=543)

Resident landlords		5
Non–resident landlords:	Individual (single lettings)	14
	Individuals (several lettings)	43
	Companies	18
	Institutions	21

(b) 1986–7 *by landlord type* (*percentages*)

	Recent mover	Established tenant
Property companies	6.1	19.7
Institutions	14.9	13.8
Relative	4.4	4.6
Employer individuals	1.3	2.4
Other individuals	74.2	59.6

Sources: (a) Todd (1988): (b) London Planning Advisory Committee (1988) and London Research Centre (1988).

let mainly as a result of personal circumstances (Todd, 1988, Paley, 1978, House of Commons Environment Committee, 1982).

Table 7.4a gives a breakdown by landlord type of lettings made in England in 1983–4. It suggests that the most important group in the market are non–resident individual landlords, most of whom let fewer than twenty units. Moreover nearly one third of lettings by this group had been acquired during the 1980s. Later evidence from London (table 7.4b) shows an even larger, and growing, preponderance of individual landlords – reflecting in particular the very rapid turnover experienced in the capital, as well as a continuing decline in institutional and company involvement in the private rented sector. Other evidence, notably Paley (1978), suggests that the resident landlord sector is also one of fairly rapid landlord turnover. Thus confidence in the market and changing attitudes to letting are likely to have a significant effect on the number of lettings coming on to the market.

Looking to the future, changes in the importance of non–commercial reasons for letting (for example, inheritance) can have some effect on total supply, but if the private rented sector is to expand (or even if the rate of decline is to slow down) it must be worthwhile for commercial landlords to enter the market and either to remain there or be replaced by other new entrants. To examine whether this is likely to occur we can look at three types of evidence: what rents and returns landlords appear able to achieve at the present time; whether these rents are adequate to make it worthwhile for current landlords to remain in the market; and, more hypothetically, what sorts of rents and returns might attract potential investors into the market. Again the main available evidence relates to London and to Sheffield.

Achievable returns and their adequacy for current landlords
The 1986/7 London Housing survey and earlier GLC evidence give us some idea of achievable rents and returns. The most important point is that rents vary enormously in ways that cannot be related to specific attributes of either dwelling or type of tenancy, given the poor quality of the data. Rents for recent movers (which can be regarded as close to market rents) were generally about 80 per cent higher than those for more established tenants and furnished rents were about 70 per cent above those for unfurnished property. Assuming lower quartile capital values we can calculate gross rates of return based on these rents. Returns on unfurnished property, which are mainly in the regulated sector and to more established tenants, ranged from between 2.2 per cent and less than 1 per cent. Rents and rates of return on furnished accommodation and particularly on property let to recent movers give a better indication of what can be achieved. Evidence from the 1986/7 survey (table 7.5) shows that on average gross rental returns were in the range of 4–4.5 per cent for all furnished lettings taken together but rose to between 4.5 per cent and 6.5 per cent for lettings to recent movers. Upper quartile and maximum returns would of course be very much higher. Evidence from the far more detailed GLC survey of 1983/4 calculated on the same basis

**Table 7.5 Rents and rates of return in furnished accommodation, London
1986/7 (£s and percentages)**

	Prices 1986/7[a] £	Mean annual rent £	Rate of return %	Rate of return Recent movers %
Central/Inner London				
Houses	65,500	2,549	3.9	4.4
Flats	54,500	2,454	4.5	6.3
Outer London				
Houses	65,000	2,590	4.0	5.6
Flats	50,000	2,122	4.2	4.8
All London				
Houses	65,000	2,573	4.0	5.6
Flats	51,000	2,339	4.5	5.1

Sources: Authors' calculations, based on data from London Planning
Advisory Committee (1988) and London Research Centre (1988).
[a]Lower quartile capital values.

suggests rather higher rates of return. Mean returns varied between 6.5
per cent and about 10 per cent while returns on lettings which could be
classified as unprotected with reasonable certainty were generally about
1 per cent higher (table 7.6). The main reason for this difference
(apart from inaccuracies in the data) is the rapid increase in capital
values in London during the intervening period. Rents in general are
always slower to adjust to such sudden changes (Harloe, 1985), but with
such a rapid turnover it may also be argued that those rents reflect
demand and that demand is inadequate to allow rents to adjust back to
1983/4 ratios.

The evidence from interviews with landlords and agents both of prime
and more average property in London is generally consistent with this
view. The responses suggest that few landlords expect to make more than
6 per cent on current capital values from rent alone. They also say that
this means that they expect to do little more than cover their costs
(including the risks of letting) from rental income. The main reason
commercial landlords give for being in the sector is the expectation of
capital gains, and most expected money increases in the value of their
property of between 12 and 15 per cent per annum (London Planning
Advisory Committee, 1988).

The second important finding from both the 1983/4 and the 1986/7
surveys was that achievable returns were clearly not adequate to stem the

Table 7.6 Rents and rates of returns (£s & percent) London 1983/4

	Prices 1983 £	Annual mean rent All furnished £	Annual mean rent Furnished (unprotected) £	Rate of return All furnished %	Rate of return Furnished (unprotected) %
All London					
Houses	45,764	4,534	5,012	9.9	11.0
Flats	32,366	2,642	2,928	8.2	9.0
Central London					
Flats	38,958	3,155	3,523	8.1	9.0
Rest of Inner London					
Houses	41,761	3,702	3,838	8.9	9.2
Flats	28,746	2,315	2,496	8.0	8.7
Outer London					
Houses	44,967	2,868	3,113	6.4	6.9
Flats	29,336	2,334	2,543	8.0	8.7

Sources: Authors' calculations based on data from 1983/4 GLC survey and the Halifax Building Society, see also Whitehead and Kleinman, (1988).

decline of the sector. Comparisons between the 1986/7 and the 1983/4 survey suggest that there had been a net loss of about 50,000 units – 15 per cent of the private rented stock over the three years. This was consistent with the estimates in the 1983/4 survey of earlier decline and implies that in net terms some 17 per cent of vacancies per annum were not being relet. Much of this decline may reflect the continuing transfer of regulated tenancies to other tenures as properties become vacant. There is no direct evidence on whether properties let on the free market and earning higher returns are being relet, except in the sense that rents are clearly inadequate to maintain, let alone expand, overall supply.

Evidence from Sheffield, where expectations of increases in capital gains are perhaps less bouyant, suggests that the rate of decline has been rather slower and that achievable rates of return have been higher. The survey by Crook and Martin (1988), showed that, among properties let in 1979, one third were no longer in the private rented sector in 1985. Of property that was relet, over half of unfurnished lettings had been transferred to the furnished sector, enough to keep the numbers of furnished lettings constant. Gross rental rates of return varied from about 5 per cent for unfurnished to 14 per cent for furnished accommodations. The range for rents net of management and maintenance, 3.4–9.5 per cent, was less, reflecting higher costs of running furnished lettings. Landlords of about 80 per cent of the furnished lettings were prepared to relet, although on average they said they would require a slightly higher return than they were receiving. Most landlords of unfurnished property were not prepared to relet but thought that returns of about 7 per cent would be sufficient to change their views.

More anecdotal evidence, for instance from Business Expansion Schemes (BES) and other surveys of market rents, suggests that gross rates of return vary from about 6–7 per cent in London to over 10 per cent on furnished property in some parts of the north and indeed 15 per cent in Glasgow (Social Housing, 1989). Returns are probably even higher for dwellings in multiple occupation where rents seem to be based more on type and number of tenants than on type of dwelling.

Overall, therefore, the evidence suggests that the majority of current lettings do not provide rents adequate to make it worthwhile for commercial landlords to relet. In the easy access, near–market sector, rents are probably adequate to ensure a stable level of supply in that part of the market, but even here there is very little evidence of expansion. Given that the traditional sector still makes up more than half of total private lettings in current conditions, the level of overall provision is likely to continue to decline.

Returns required by new investors

The final question is, therefore, what rents and rates of return might be necessary to bring entirely new investors into the market under current conditions. One thing we do know is that the earlier assured tenancy scheme was not seen as providing an adequate return without additional tax benefits (Kemp, 1988a). Other than this we are mainly dependent on anecdotal evidence and that observable from BES schemes (for example, London Research Centre, 1988 and Social Housing, 1989). Landlords and agents in London appear to require at least 5–6 per cent to cover costs of lettings with an overall gross monetary return including capital gains of between 15 and 20 per cent. If actual capital gains fell below the landlords' rather high expectations the required return from rent alone would presumably increase. This picture is consistent with the Sheffield evidence where expected capital gains are lower and rental returns at least 7 per cent on unfurnished lettings and nearer 15 per cent on higher risk, higher cost, furnished accommodation as required. Moreover the relatively low rental return required on unfurnished accommodation probably comes from the traditional style of landlord and is likely to be well below that necessary to induce additional investment. Evidence from BES schemes suggests that rental returns of 8–15 per cent (rather lower in the south) are necessary to induce individuals to invest even with large–scale tax advantages. Finally, interviews with financial institutions suggest that, given prevailing perceptions of risk, currently available rents are inadequate to bring large–scale finance into the market (London Planning Advisory Committee, 1988).

What level of provision?

Using the data from the London survey we can compare the rents necessary to achieve desired returns with rents currently being paid in the near–market sector. We can then ask in general terms what factors might change to bring demand and supply into line. In so doing we can attempt to give an indication of the potential size of the sector and its role in the housing market.

Table 7.7 gives an estimate of the average rents necessary to give a 6 per cent gross return on capital values for the lowest quartile of dwellings in London compared to rents observed in the furnished sector in 1986/7. Such a return appears to be roughly what landlords and managers say they are trying to achieve given their expectations of capital gains. As such it is probably the minimum return necessary to keep the size of even the easy access sector in being.

The comparison suggests that average rents in London might have to rise by between 30 and 50 per cent in order to achieve even these gross returns. Many landlords are therefore not obtaining their perceived required return.

Moreover, even at existing rent levels, 35 per cent of tenants were paying more than 20 per cent of their income in rent. This suggests that demand may not even be adequate to maintain existing levels of supply. If rents rise towards those required by potential landlords, higher income households and those with other opportunities would go elsewhere; lower income households would double up, more simply not form, or move

Table 7.7 Comparison of required and actual rents, London 1986/7

	Current mean rents (furnished accommodation)		
	All tenants	Recent movers	Rents providing 6% gross return
	£pa	£pa	£pa
Central/Inner London			
Houses	2,549	2,882	3,925
Flats	2,454	3,344	3,265
Outer London			
Houses	2,590	3,640	3,885
Flats	2,122	2,400	3,034
All London			
Houses	2,573	3,640	3,860
Flats	2,339	2,600	3,119

Sources: See table 7.5.

out to lower price accommodation. The baseline scenario in London is therefore of a smaller sector than at present with supply concentrated in the provision of dwellings in multiple occupation where returns are highest.

There is even less direct evidence about the position outside London. There are undoubtedly many areas where the general picture appears to be one of balance so the immediate effect of deregulation can be expected to be small. What is however clear (for example, from data on housing associations, see Randolph and Lewis, 1988) is that throughout the country new investment would produce rents far in excess of what people would be prepared to pay for out of their own resources. For instance, in Sheffield, housing association cost rent levels would be over £4,000 per annum, while in central London they would be at least double this level. This compares with observed assured tenancy (that is, market) rents on equivalent property of little more than half the Sheffield estimate (Department of Environment, 1986).

The main implication of our analysis so far is that if the future is like the past it is unlikely that the size of even the easy access sector will significantly increase. As the traditional sector must continue to decline, deregulation will be associated (as it was after the last attempt in 1957) with a lower level of provision of privately rented accommodation.

Change in incentives to supply

There are of course many reasons why the future may not be like the past. Most obviously on the supply side current estimates of required returns may be higher than those necessary in a more secure environment where investors feel they are in control of their assets. In other words the threat of regulation may have kept potential investors out of the market and ensured that those who did supply wanted returns high enough to cover their perceived high risks. This position cannot be changed overnight. Current anecdotal evidence suggests that financial institutions are not yet prepared to risk any large-scale involvement – indeed even housing associations are still having to pay somewhat over the local authority rate for funds, however well secured against current equity (Housing Corporation, 1988a).

Even if funds were to be forthcoming, investors are sure to require a significant risk premium for a long time to come. The most obvious reasons for this include: (i) the political uncertainty with respect to rents and security of tenure; (ii) the fact that, given expected rent levels, a large proportion of the return must come from capital gains (either monetary or real). The housing market has provided a bonanza in the past but there are reasons to suggest that prices may already include some over-optimism about the future; (iii) the difficulties of diversification against specific risks using traditional financing methods. In particular, private renting has always been provided mainly by small individual landlords who cannot diversify effectively. A revived sector would need a new breed of landlord splitting financing, risk and management and involving the development of new types of security; (iv) most importantly, compared with for example, commercial property, it is difficult to be sure that rent income will rise even in line with general incomes. On the one hand operating costs of supply are labour intensive and involve specific skills. On the other, trends in income distribution suggest that those at the lower end of the income scale are likely to do worse than the average over the next few years. Stable and growing rent income therefore depends on attracting long–term tenants with at least average expectations with respect to income growth.

These factors, taken together with the rate of return currently available in other parts of the finance market and the expected rate of inflation, suggest that overall returns net of management and maintenance costs would have to be at least 10–12 per cent and maybe more. This would imply differential rental returns in different areas related to expectations about house price increases. In areas of bouyant expectations a large proportion of the return might be expected to come from capital growth. In more depressed regions where, of course, capital values and therefore rents would be much lower in absolute terms, a much higher proportion would come from rental income.

We separate out the costs of management, maintenance and

Table 7.8 Management and maintenance costs (£s per annum)

	Inner London	Provinces
New build		
Maintenance	260	233
Decoration	67	63
Management	245	203
	572	**499**
Rehabilitated		
Maintenance	490	454
Decoration	67	63
Management	277	247
	834	**764**
Sheltered units (rehab.)		
Maintenance	490	454
Decoration	67	63
Management	347	287
	904	**804**
Higher management allowance	106	106
	1,010	**910**

Source: Housing Corporation, (1988b).

administration because they play a different role. If they are not covered by rent income it may still be worth the landlord's while to own property in order to obtain the capital growth but, instead of letting it, it will be better to keep the property off the market. Moreover these costs are also not proportional to asset values but rather depend upon the type of property, the type of tenure and perhaps the specific type of tenant.

We have very little direct evidence of operating costs in the private rented sector, partly because for small landlords they are often implicit rather than direct payments.

One possible approach is to ask how much it costs housing associations to run different types of property. This is directly relevant as financial institutions and others who may be prepared to finance private renting will generally not wish to organise their own management. They are likely to turn to housing associations or to managing agents (who can be expected to charge even higher fees). Table 7.8 shows levels of management and maintenance costs allowed by the housing corporation. These suggest management and maintenance costs can form a very high proportion of current rents. They also imply that while management costs are higher in London they form a very much smaller proportion of values and that the operating costs of short stay lettings for particularly problematic types of tenant may be almost twice those for modern housing on long term lets. Even this ratio is almost certainly an underestimate as associations do not, in the main, house many of the more mobile types of tenant found in the privately rented sector. Indeed the Sheffield study suggests that the landlords of more risky high turnover furnished lets require twice the return of landlords involved in more traditional furnished lettings.

While these figures are very rough, they do suggest that returns on rental alone would seem to be at the lower end of the possible scale necessary to attract potential landlords and especially if institutional finance is to be made available in the medium term. On top of this there would have to be elements covering higher costs of rapid turnover and more management intensive tenants. Finally, expected capital gains of well over the rate of inflation would be required. Overall 12–15 per cent would seem to be a minimum requirement.

In making these estimates we should stress that this rate is considerably lower than that which potential investors currently quote. Significant flows of finance at these sorts of rates would only be forthcoming if it could be demonstrated that there was adequate demand from desirable tenants and that the risks of letting have been reduced considerably in comparison to past experience.

Consumer decisions
The chance that tenants prepared to pay these rents will be forthcoming in large numbers seems, at least in current conditions, to be unlikely. As we have discussed above, in London employed households do make up the majority of the easy access sector but even here many are on relatively

low incomes and can only pay because they group together; the costs of letting are therefore fairly high. Moreover, the sector as a whole is still declining. In Sheffield the majority of new tenants are students or the unemployed with very limited capacity to pay – and again there is no sign of expansion.

So again determining factors would have to change to induce demand. For the employed the main option is owner–occupation. A household about to choose takes into account four elements: rent versus expected outgoing on the owner–occupied dwelling, expected capital gains in owner–occupation compared with other investment opportunities, comparative transactions costs and the types of property available.

At the present time first–time buyers' mortgage outgoings range from as little as £1,250 a year in the north to £5,000 a year in Greater London. North of the Severn/Wash line these appear to be roughly comparable to or perhaps a little higher than rents. In the south, and especially London, they are generally higher, although well below observed maximum rents. Throughout the country, but notably in London, the quality and quantity of what is being obtained is far less in the private rented sector than in owner–occupation. Moreover, over the last two decades owner–occupiers have made large real capital gains, far greater than those available on low–risk investments elsewhere. A detailed comparison would also take account of relative management and maintenance costs and transactions costs. However, until recently, expected capital gains have been enough to offset any differential costs to owner–occupiers except for those who require accommodation for only a short time.

Underlying these comparisons are other elements including relative expectations of net capital gains between owner–occupiers, landlords and tenants, relative access to capital and evaluations of risk, and the relative tax position of owner–occupiers and landlords plus tenants, as well as attitudes to the essential jointness of owner–occupation and the landlord/tenant relationship (Whitehead and Kleinman, 1986).

The most important point here is that while higher expectations of capital gains reduce required rents, they also reduce the costs to owner–occupiers in the same way. They therefore do not generally shift consumer choice from owning to renting. Perceptions of potential gains may also differ, because of different information, because owner–occupiers may be more optimistic and because the market may value tenanted property differently even when market rents can be charged.

With respect to access to capital, owner–occupiers are worse off in terms of interest relief because of the £30,000 ceiling. On the other hand, at least until last year, they probably paid relatively low interest rates. The most important aspect in the long term is the market's perception of relative risk which certainly currently favours owner–occupation over landlordism although this could be modified in the 1990s.

With respect to tax, owner–occupiers benefit from the lack of tax on imputed income (only partially offset by the lack of tax relief on mortgages over £30,000) and from the lack of capital gains tax. In addition, landlords still lose from the treatment of housing as a perpetual asset and tax allowances limited to property income and to marketed management costs. Overall, the tax system still favours owner–occupation very significantly and is likely to continue to do so unless more subsidies to landlords are introduced.

It can also be argued that the relationship between a profit–seeking landlord and a tenant is inherently more complex and costly to organise than the jointness of owner–occupation. If so, renting may be an inferior product for most tenants even if a similar range of property were available (Whitehead, 1979). This is borne out by declines in the commercial private rented sectors in many other advanced countries, including those with preferential tax treatments (Harloe, 1985).

Finally, there is the question of relative costs of management and maintenance. Owner–occupiers may use their own time and skills as well as choose the timing of expenditure. Landlords and managers have the benefits of specialisation and large scale, but tenants have little incentive to minimise wear and tear. Moreover, owner–occupiers almost certainly underestimate the costs they bear as most are not marketed, so the choice is biased towards owner–occupation.

Overall, therefore, it is not surprising that the majority of households expecting to remain in their accommodation for more than a year or two choose owner–occupation if they can. The equation is shifting, and would shift more if a wider range of private rented property became available. But that is a chicken and egg problem. At the present time potential landlords are not convinced that suitable tenants will be forthcoming and thus are unlikely to change their behaviour simply in response to deregulation.

The position at the bottom end of the market is very different. People have few choices and these choices are becoming more restricted as access to the social sector declines. However, capacity to pay depends to a greater extent on the availability and generosity of housing benefit. At the present time ministers have promised that housing benefit will be available to fund the shift to market rents, but it would be a foolish landlord, or investor, who would expect that position to remain unchanged. Moreover, modifications in the housing benefit system mean that the majority of those in work will either be wholly dependent on their own resources (and therefore likely to enter owner–occupation where possible) or will be at a level where the 65 per cent taper on rents applies. The effect of this rate of clawback is to limit severely lower income households' capacity to pay (see, for example, Hills, 1988).

Thus, further up the market, the demand for private renting depends upon choice and that choice still favours owner–occupation except for easy access accommodation. At the bottom end, the viability of the sector depends almost wholly upon the extent of generosity of the housing benefit system. Government can fund a viable private rented sector but within current constraints only through large and increasing subsidies to tenants and/or supply subsidies to landlords. Without such changes the private rented sector will continue to decline in terms of total numbers. The easy access subsector will probably expand but it will take considerably more than the 1988 Housing Act to ensure change.

A viable private rented sector?
There are now fewer constraints on the free operation of the privately rented sector. If there are willing buyers and sellers then a market of some sort will appear. To a significant extent such a market already exists in the easy access sector.

The market must however, given past experience, appear risky, especially to institutional investors. It will take time to persuade new landlords to come into the market at any significant scale. Longer–term involvement must anyway depend upon demand.

Demand depends upon capacity to pay as well as on the other options available. At the bottom end of the income scale, especially among those not in the labour force, the relevant choice is with social housing and the capacity to pay will come mainly from social security. Further up the income scale the tax system, relative evaluations of risk and capital gains, relative operating costs and even the nature of the landlord/tenant relationship all continue to favour owner–occupation except for mobile households. This is not a strong basis from which to build the revival of the private rented sector.

There are three major areas where the operation of the private rented sector bears significantly on the macroeconomy. The aspect where most interest has been concentrated is with respect to labour mobility. Here, undoubtedly, choices are distorted, but the existence of a private rented sector would not alone make it possible for workers to afford to move to where the jobs are. Moreover, that part of the market has always been relatively unconstrained. It will expand somewhat and operate more effectively under deregulation, but far more basic changes would be needed if private renting is to play a significantly larger part.

Much more important in practice is the relationship between housing benefit, private rents and the incentive to find employment. Market rents of the type discussed here would ensure that households were affected by housing benefit clawback (65 per cent rent, 20 per cent rates) both on low incomes and quite a long way up the earnings scale. The incentive to work, or indeed to earn an extra £1, are therefore significantly reduced. Private renting is only a part of this problem, as rents will also rise in the housing association and local authority sectors. The underlying problem is that of housing costs and standards in relation to income, that is, it is a question of affordability and income redistribution rather than the specifics of ownership and organisation within the rented market.

The final important relationship between the private rented sector and the more macro economy is that relating to the finance market. Institutional finance at present is hardly involved in residential property. Such involvement would in principle be valuable, both for the finance market and for the independent rented sector. However, the conditions are not yet adequately favourable, at least in the private sector, for such a market to develop. It would certainly involve new types of securities and new relationships between financing and management within the sector. For the moment, however, the main source of finance will continue to be individual investors playing a direct role in provision.

Note

[1]Data on private renting are poor. The 1981 Census is the last fairly accurate count, although even there the errors would have been far larger than for other tenures. Moreover, the definition of private renting is not precise. At the margins bed and breakfast accommodation and, to a lesser extent, hostels may sometimes be included and sometimes not, depending notably on the current form of social security benefits.

8 The national economy, regional imbalances and housing policies
Duncan Maclennan

Introduction

This volume is based upon a set of conference papers which were presented, under the supervision of the National Institute, as part of the Joseph Rowntree Memorial Trust's programme of work on the United Kingdom housing finance and subsidy system. This programme, like most research on housing economics in Britain, has focussed upon a series of sectoral and regional case studies. Sectoral studies naturally reflect the marked differences in subsidy levels and systems across the main tenure sectors. Regional and local case studies have been emphasised in the Programme as the initial incidence and final impacts of subsidy arrangements evolve in the context of local housing markets. The spatially fixed nature of housing land and the existing housing stock mean that, even if econometric estimates were ready to hand, 'national' supply elasticities would have little relevance to many of the questions raised in housing debates. Similarly localised or regionalised demand preferences operating in conjunction with mobility costs result in housing demand having a local or non–portable component.

Housing market analyses which ignore the geographic compartmentalisation of housing and labour markets within the national economy may well be reductionist to the point of throwing the baby out with the bathwater. The chapters in this volume have generally avoided this criticism. However a concern must remain that in moving from national, aspatial, models to a more disaggregated focus, a rather casual geography is being utilised and potentially very limited price data is employed. Standard economic planning regions may contain well defined, separated housing and labour markets with different experiences. Aggregation biases and spuriously high regression coefficients may arise. For instance I have, in the early 1980s, produced a house price inflation model for Scotland (and other regions) which was, then, econometrically acceptable. This was completed with the full knowledge that Aberdeen, Edinburgh and Glasgow then had quite different local housing market experiences. I suspect that the regions used, *seriatim*, in this volume will not long represent an acceptable level of disaggregation.

The observations of the previous paragraph should, in no way, be seen as an argument against the development of rigorous macro to micro models of the British housing system. In the micro–oriented Rowntree programme we are conscious of the housing sector relevance of truly macroeconomic variables such as interest and exchange rates and of national policies for more locally generated phenomena, such as unemployment and inflation.

We need to understand much more about national to local (and *vice versa*) transmission mechanisms in the economy. Unfortunately, the housing and housing finance sectors (in spite of their aggregate importance in consumer spending, fixed capital formation, employment and retail capital markets) have not been subject to sustained research by the British economics profession. Shifting involvements have arisen in the past in relation to residential building cycles, house price inflation, financial deregulation but, as is reflected in the naively weak 'housing' sectors of national economic models, there has been no steadily evolving set of insights and few experienced researchers. Hopefully this volume may spark such an interest. It is not without irony that it is in the developing countries, as was ably demonstrated by Buckley and Mayo in their presentation to the conference, that there is a willingness to address the spatial, temporal and inter–sectoral effects of housing in the national economy.

This volume has touched upon a number of housing/macroeconomy interactions, although it was primarily focussed upon the regional imbalance problems now so evident in the United Kingdom. The bulk of this endpiece also focusses upon this critical question, but it is pertinent to mention related topics which urgently require attention.

Classical economists seldom neglected land (including housing) in their grand models. But do we now pay sufficient attention to the national economic aspects of land and real estate? I think not. We have little understanding of how rising housing and land prices are 'caused' nor how they affect national economic competitiveness. Britain, through both public and private sectors, spends an internationally high to average proportion of GNP on real estate, but are these expenditures translated into output, rather than prices, as effectively as in our European allies and competitors? In the British academic tradition we have largely passed investigation of land and housing issues to town planners and social administrators and, in consequence, our economic knowlege base is limited.

Meen, in Chapter 3, has examined the critical question of changing
financial regimes, but are we yet in any position to say how post–1986
mortgage and capital market deregulation has affected the economy or,
looking to the future, how 1992 will internationalise land and housing
finance circuits?   Are we able to say, as Ed Mills and others have asked
in the United States, whether tax and subsidy systems lead to 'too much'
housing expenditure in Britain?   Have we anything at all to say about the
changing efficiency of the construction sector and how the land planning
system mediates price and output effects?   At our conference Evans (see
Comment on Chapter 6) pointed out how the British housing system spends
billions annually stimulating demand and how the planning system
restricts flows of supply.   Intuitively I agree with Alan Evans, but hard
evidence will be needed to change the policies, indeed philosophies, of
central and local governments.

Other issues merit our attention.   Clearly we need to understand
much more about the economic causes and consequences of equity withdrawal
and at present research is focussed upon measurement issues.   As the
national tenure share of owner occupation and real house prices continue
(in the long term) to rise, then equity withdrawal and housing dominated
inheritances become more important in shaping wealth redistribution and
spending patterns.   Stored housing assets may be extremely important in
coping with the consequences of ageing which confronts us to the year
2000. Recent contributions in the United States, have stressed the
potentially major housing and macroeconomic consequences of the baby boom
bust.   Though they were not a major focus in this volume, the recent
paper by Dicks (1988a) highlights why they should be central to our
concerns.   Indeed, it may be that unless we have a clearer understanding
of financial sector changes, taxation effects, inheritance, equity
withdrawal and the supply side, then we will not be able to sensibly
comprehend the regional imbalance problems examined at length in this
volume.

The preceding paragraphs have emphasised the importance of a renewed
commitment to macroeconomic thinking on British housing issues. However,
it is also fair to suggest that microeconomic analysis has done little to
foster appropriate theoretical interactions.   Locational analyses, tenure
choice and public policy studies have dominated the United Kingdom
housing economics agenda in the 1980s.   Labour market and housing
analysts, with contributions to this volume being important exceptions,
have had few interactions in spite of the similarity of the intellectual
puzzles which confront them.   There has been an almost complete absence
of supply–side analysis, changes in housing quality have been ignored and
there are few robust estimates of depreciation rates and, in spite of a
recognition of the asset attributes of housing, there are few studies of
how housing market expectations are formed and revised.   At the urban
scale, where appropriate price data banks do exist, there has been no
analysis of whether rational or adaptive expectations best explain
observed price patterns.   Housing market analysis, in Britain, has
absorbed few of the techniques of financial market analyses.

The Joseph Rowntree Memorial Trust housing finance programme, and especially its six local–regional case studies, provides an important opportunity to remedy some of these deficiences of past micro–economic approaches.

National–regional imbalances

The National Institute meeting has pointed up the importance of housing market imbalances within the United Kingdom. Research problems and possibilities have been identified which merit further detailed scrutiny. The complexity and localised nature of housing and labour markets have been identified.

Different spatial fixities for different factors of production (that is, capital, land and different labour market groups), along with externalities, lie at the core of the problem. Intertemporal shifts in the pattern of labour demand and supply create shifts in the demand for housing across areas with differential price effects as well as congestion externalities. In turn, changing house prices and rents shift subsidy patterns and incomes and wage rates, albeit Muellbauer (Chapter 4, major effect) and Hughes and McCormick (Chapter 6, modest effect) do not yet offer a consensus view of this point. Clearly a major exercise in disentanglement, requiring good data, appropriate spatial specifications as well as sophisticated econometrics, will be required to produce real understanding.

The regional pattern of potential labour market entrants has changed over the last two decades, with endogenous population growth in the southern metropolitan areas increasing. South–east pressures will grow even without increased in–migration. Regional patterns of retirals will also vary and the end of job career housing move will have an increasing bearing upon the house price consequences of further growth in southern Britain. Even if retiring owners take their capital gains and relocate north and west, and this effect of returning Anglos is already evident in Scottish housing markets, then a major problem exists insofar as retiring council tenants may have little price incentive to move elsewhere.

Imbalances in potential labour supply, by skill sector and geographic location, may be a growing problem in Britain in the 1990s. It is important to note that whilst north–south imbalances dominate the present discussion, that intra–urban or intra–regional imbalances may be equally problematic. The last decade has demonstrated clearly that unskilled and semi–skilled workers are more likely to encounter redundancies and longer unemployment spells than workers with higher human capital levels. And of course such groups are disproportionately represented in the locally segmented social housing sector. For instance, in a recent Glasgow study, the true unemployment rate within peripheral housing schemes was measured at 38 per cent for adult males and of those in the labour force 55 per cent had experienced at least one spell of unemployment in the last five years. Contraction in traditional industries explained the pattern of job losses. The low resources of these households precluded private sector housing solutions. Local lettings policies would have prevented moves to Edinburgh let alone Epping. Similar problems exist within most northern regions.

The emerging pattern of labour demand in Britain over the last decade has reinforced the locational attractions of southern Britain. There are few reasons to believe why the Channel tunnel and 1992 will not reinforce this pattern. For the last five years housing ministers have argued, through less strongly over time, that rising housing costs in pressured areas will increase wages and, in turn, induce decentralistion to lower cost locations. Recent experience south of Sheffield may partly justify this view, but this may be nothing more than an extension of the great 'wen' rather than regional decentralisation. Firms have expanded housing allowances to workers to relocate to pressured areas but this has only marginally assuaged pressures on wages. However, many firms in pressured areas may have price making powers nationally, and internationally exchange rates may adjust rather than have firms make conscious relocation decisions. Of course this set of problems might have been somewhat ameliorated if government had not set its face so firmly against regional policies. I am not, of course, arguing for the often inefficient policies of the 1950–80 period, but rather that in the face of growing congestion effects in the south that government must urgently consider what kind of regional Britain it wants in the 21st Century.

At the very least the government should critically review how much of the civil service needs to be in London. I believe, for instance, that the huge Environment Ministry would be better broken up into regional agencies located in the areas they serve. Any other volunteers? Or we could ask, now that the threat of Napoleon has subsided, why such a large proportion of the armed services are located within 50 miles of London.

I suspect that the real push to government, in this respect, will not come from the high unemployment, Labour–held constituencies of the north. Rather, unless more 'brownfield' rehabilitation sites can be found and developed within the south–east, the reaction may stem from the increasing 'green' concerns of the 'true–blue' home counties. Rapid south–east growth, affordable housing costs and quality environments/continuing green belts are, ultimately, mutually exclusive objectives. If firms can ignore the traffic congestion consequences and environmental consequences of green belt removal, southern Members of Parliament cannot. Patterns of regional labour demand, 50 years after the Barlow report, will be central to the United Kingdom political agenda in the next decade.

Most discussions of economic growth–led housing imbalances focus upon inflation and congestion effects in the fast growth city. But fast growth and housing imbalance involves a mix of gainers and losers. Voluntary emigrants may take housing and land capital gains and trade down and out of London. Non–movers may incur holding gains, and this may have wealth effects on consumption, equity withdrawal and so on. New entrants are likely losers, although high housing costs may help secure a more secure long–term labour market position. There is little doubt that there is growing awareness that current housing subsidies, for instance Housing Support Grant per capita, tax reliefs per head and Housing Benefit per capita are now higher and growing faster in London and the south–east than in northern regions. Northern residents with reduced job opportunities are increasingly unsympathetic to the subsidisation of housing costs in prosperous locations. Why subsidise residential location and not job location? This is not an unfair question for northern residents of the United Kingdom to pursue.

Aside from courteous disquiet, there may be other negative effects on peripheral regions and over different time periods. In the very short run and lasting into the long term, price and rent rises in the congested region may quickly thwart necessary labour migration away from declining regions and industries. Sheer availability, rather than price, constraints may be critical in the rental sector. In consequence, if dependency and disadvantage emerge, they are borne and their externalities reinforced in peripheral regions. Spatial separation is, of course, a useful device for tolerating higher levels of inequality and, in the British system, minimising its political consequences.

In the medium term, southern home–owners may be discouraged from locating north as part of a temporary career move. Not only will the real value of their housing capital be less than maximal but, reflecting long–term wealth inequalities, there may be a genuine shortage of high value housing and house prices may rise and begin to choke–off shifts to the peripheral areas. It may take relatively few job moves of southern executives to northern cities to raise markedly local house prices. There is evidence of this effect as far north as the Scottish cities. This may provide some hints as to why regional prices have relativity cycles. Most models explain why the south inflates first, but few address why, in the past, relativities are restored after several years (though there is now some suspicion that relativities have permanently changed, even if in 1989 the north has begun to recover vis–à–vis the south).

When southern house price inflation is sustained into the medium term and spills over into wage costs and the general price level, then a government policy reaction is likely. In Britain with more home owners than ever, each holding historic record levels of real housing debt, it is unsurprising that the Chancellor regards higher interest and mortgage rate rises (and Britain relies on rapidly variable rate mortgages to an extent unmatched elsewhere) as being a key means of curtailing consumer spending and house price inflation. In the peripheral regions where mortgage and price–to–income ratios are lower than in the south, house prices may continue to increase, thus narrowing the north–south gap. But the key issue for the northern regions is whether the policy scenario to curtail consumer spending forestalls the diffusion of economic growth to these regions. If there is a tendency for the south to export house price inflation but not economic prosperity, then the southern housing market pressures may have very negative long–run effects on northern regions.

The above paragraphs are full of questions and conditional statements. They are intended to stress that in further research on housing, regions and the macroeconomy we must stress a truly national and not solely southern standpoint. Further, they stress that housing, environmental and industrial development policies must be consistent.

Housing policy issues

I presume that I was asked to make these concluding comments not as the only contributor to the conference (Hughes excepted) who holds his housing assets north of Sheffield, but rather as a housing analyst. It may therefore be pertinent to conclude with a number of remarks on how present housing policies affect present imbalances.

I have already noted the perverse regional (but not necesarily individual) pattern of housing subsidies in Britain. As a consequence of the last decade of change in housing and economic policies, per capita subsidies are higher in London and the south–east than in the northern regions. Given the supply constraints in the south, present demand–side subsidies, especially owner tax concessions, may be largely wasted and passed as 'economic rents' to real–estate owners.

Private sector supply systems may be in need of a thorough overhaul. The previous paragraphs suggest that land is released too slowly (in relation to the pace of economic change) in pressured and depressed regions alike. In the 1980s, subsidised public and private improvement grant investment has switched from new construnction to modernisation, amidst a sharply reduced overall public investment total. There is little doubt that well–used rehabilitation expenditure has had a major impact upon neighbourhoods in northern cities, most notably Glasgow. Indeed, in the latter case strategic revitalisation has produced an urban core capable of competing for mobile service sector jobs. Intensely pursued housing reinvestment policies can, clearly, shift the location of the national economic base and, allied to enterprise–oriented local economic development policies, may offer a broad hint of how to secure better balanced Britain with higher quality cities, in both north and south Britain. But these policies are expensive: so far Glasgow's 'miracle' has cost the Exchequer close to £1.5 billion over fifteen years.

The government has set its face against the provision of new council housing, the adjustment mechanism of the 1960s and 1970s as the private rental sector declined. I have much sympathy for the government's attempt to demonopolise municipal housing and to raise management efficiency and effectiveness. However, by 1990, councils will not be able to subsidise housing from local taxes and the Housing Support Grant, outside of London, has largely disappeared. In that context it would be fairer if councils were freed of their investment restrictions and allowed to invest subject to competitive pressures.

Before allowing such steps, government must, however, have a much clearer view of where it wants social housing to be and make an honest assessment of how much is required. The tightening of the British housing system in the 1980s (see Chapter 7) is a fairly predictable outcome of policy decisions. A similar, strategic view on housing association investment is required. Much housing association activity shifted northwards and into rehabilitation in the 1980s, precisely at the period when homelessness and low income affordability problems strengthened in the south. Failure on the part of government to provide clear signals on where housing issues are to be solved and their vacillation on the required level of investment merely confuses the housing corporation and creates strife across regional housing lobbies. Nicholas Ridley was, in my view, asking an entirely pertinent question when he queried whether it was not better to house the homeless in their source regions rather than London, and this may extend to the unemployable and the elderly. But the responding question to Mr Ridley is, what geographic pattern of affordable social rental housing is most consistent with the government's views on congestion in London, threatened green belts in the south and tolerable levels of regional inequalities? Like, I suspect, Mr Ridley, I believe that an extension of market financing and allocation mechanisms will have major long–term benefits for the British housing system. But even the strictest interpreters and disciples of Hayek are aware that urban externalities and confused price signals which, as noted above, underpin the housing market imbalance issue, require some coordinated information device to resolve such issues.

In their well argued contribution, Whitehead and Kleinman (Chapter 7) stressed the likely limited contribution of private rental sector deregulation to the resolution of these mobility issues. Tax incentives and finance arrangements in the United Kingdom are likely to mean that private rental housing will never become a mainstream, long–term tenure for most households. Unless government were to abandon the favoured status of owner occupation and social rented housing, rental sector deregulation will only be significant for younger mobile households. There are already signs that new measures have stimulated rental investment, but mainly in northern cities. And this change may reduce regional imbalance problems. However, in the high–rent, shortage context of southern Britain, investment levels will remain modest. Further tax concessions will only exacerbate property shortages and only a much reformed housing benefit system would make new private rental development widely affordable to young, mobile populations.

There is little doubt that lack of coherent research in this area has prevented the emergence of an understanding of the issues involved. At the same time, the problem has been confounded by the failure of governments, central and local, to confront the policy issues involved. Clearly, public sector investment strategies could be more appropriately designed to cope with these complex problems and a great deal of current subsidy is largely wasted in price rather than output effects, not least because of our land planning system. Britain, even a more market oriented Britain, could do much better into the 21st Century.

References

Alberts, W.W. (1962), 'Business cycles, residential construction and the mortgage market', *Journal of Political Economy*, June.

Anderson, G.J. and Hendry, D.F. (1984), 'An econometric model of United Kingdom building societies', *Oxford Bulletin of Economics and Statistics*, **46**, no.3, August, 185–210.

Askari, M. (1986), 'A disequilibrium econometric study of the Canadian mortgage market', *Applied Economics*, **18**, 399–410.

Audit Commission (1989), *Housing the Homeless: The Local Authority Role*, London, The Audit Commission.

Bovaird, A., Harloe, M. and Whitehead, C.M.E. (1985), 'Private rented housing, its current role', *Journal of Social Policy*, January.

Bover, O., Muellbauer, J. and Murphy, A. (1988), 'Housing wages and UK labour markets', Discussion paper no.268, London, Centre for Economic Policy Research.

Brown, A.J. (1972), *The Framework of Regional Economics in the United Kingdom*, Cambridge University Press.

Buckley, R. and Ermisch, J. (1982), 'Government policy and house prices in the United Kingdom: an econometric analysis', *Oxford Bulletin of Economics and Statistics*, **44**, 273–304.

Burridge, P. and Gordon, I. (1981), 'Unemployment in the British metropolitan labour areas', *Oxford Economic Papers*, **33**, 274–97.

Cheshire, P.C., Sheppard, S. and Hooper, A. (1985), 'The economic consequences of the British planning system', University of Reading discussion paper no. 29 in Urban and Regional Economics.

143

Congdon, T. (1982), 'The coming book in housing credit', L. Messel and Co. research report, June.

Conway, J. and Kemp, P. (1985), *Bed and Breakfast: Slum Housing of the Eighties*, London, SHAC.

Crook, A.D.H. and Martin, G. (1988), 'Property speculation, local authority policy and the decline of private rented housing in the 1980s: A case study of Sheffield', in Kemp, P. (Ed.) (1988*b*), *op. cit.*

David, E.P. and Saville, I.D. (1982), 'Mortgage lending and the housing market', *Bank of England Quarterly Bulletin*, **22**, 390–8.

Davidson, J.E.H., Hendry, D.F., Srba, F. and Yeo, S. (1978), 'Econometric modelling of the aggregate time series relationship between consumer expenditure and income in the UK', *Economic Journal*, **88**, 661–92.

Department of the Environment (1986), *Assured Tenancies: Monitoring Exercise 1986*, London, Dept of Environment.

Department of the Environment (1987a), *Housing: The Government's Proposals*, Cm 214, London, HMSO.

Department of the Environment (1987b), *The Private Rented Sector: The Government's Legislative Proposals*, London, Dept of Environment.

Department of the Environment (1987c), *Deregulation of the Private Rented Sector: Consultation paper on the Implications of Housing Benefit*, London, Dept of Environment.

Department of the Environment (1988a), *Housing and Construction Statistics* 1977 – 1988, London, HMSO.

Department of the Environment (1988b), *English House Condition Survey* 1986, London, HMSO.

Dicks, M.J. (1988a), 'The demographics of housing demand; household formation and the growth of owner–occupation', Bank of England Discussion Paper, no. 32, July.

Dicks, M.J. (1988b), 'The interest elasticity of consumers' expenditure', Bank of England Technical Paper no. 20, December.

Drayson, S.J. (1985), 'The housing finance market: recent growth in perspective', *Bank of England Quarterly Bulletin*, March.

Ebrill, L.P., Possen, U.M. (1982), 'Inflation and the taxation of equity in corporations and owner–occupied housing', *Journal of Money, Credit and Banking*, **XIV**, no.1, February, 33–47.

Evans, A.W. (1983), 'The determination of the price of land', *Urban Studies*, **20**, 119–29.

Evans, A.W. (1987), *House Prices and Land Prices in the South East – A Review*, London, The House Builders Federation.

Evans, A.W. (1988), 'No room! No room! The costs of the British town and country planning system'. Occasional Paper 79, Institute for Economic Affairs.

Fair, R.C. (1972), 'Disequilibrium in housing models', *Journal of Finance*, **27**, no.2, 207–21.

Fair, R.C. and Jaffee, D.M. (1972), 'Methods of estimation for markets in disequilibrium', *Econometrica*, **40**, no. 3, 497–514.

Fisher, R.M. and Siegman, C.J. (1972), 'Patterns of housing experience during periods of credit restraint in industrialised countries', *Journal of Finance Proceedings*, **XXVII**, no.2, 193–206.

Gleave, D. and Palmer, D. (1979), 'Mobility constraints and unemployment mismatch: an analysis of structural changes in the housing market and their consequences on job migration', WN546, London, Centre for Environmental Studies.

Goodhart, C. (1986), 'Financial innovation and monetary control', *Oxford Review of Economic Policy*, **2**, Winter, 89.

Gordon, I.R. (1982), 'The analysis of motivation specific migration streams', *Environment and Planning A*, **14**, 5–20.

Gordon, I.R. (1985a), 'The cyclical sensitivity of regional employment and unemployment differentials', *Regional Studies*, **19**, 95–110.

Gordon, I.R. (1985b), 'The cyclical interaction between regional migration, employment and unemployment', *Scottish Journal of Political Economy*, **32**, 135–58.

Gordon, I.R. (1987), 'The structural element in regional unemployment', in Gordon, I. (Ed.), *Unemployment, Regions and Labour Markets: Reactions to Recession*, Pion.

Gordon, I.R. (1988), 'Evaluating the effects of employment changes on local unemployment', *Regional Studies*, **22**, 135–47.

Gough, T.J. (1975), 'Phases of British private housebuilding and the supply of mortgage credit', *Applied Economics*, **7**, 213–22.

Greater London Council (1986), *Private Tenants in London: the GLC Survey 1983–84*, London, GLC.

Green, A.E. (1988), 'The north–south divide in Great Britain: an examination of the evidence', *Transactions*, Institute of British Geographers, **13**, 179–98.

Grigson, W.S. (1986), *House Prices in Perspective: A Review of South East Evidence*, London, London and South East Regional Planning Conference.

Guttentag, J.M. (1961), 'The short cycle in residential construction, 1946–59', *American Economic Review*, **LI**, no.3, June, 275–98.

Hall, S.G. (1986), 'An application of the Granger and Engle two–step estimation procedure to United Kingdom aggregate wage data', *Oxford Bulletin of Economics and Statistics*, **48**, no.3, 229–40.

Hamnett and Randolf (1988), 'The residualisation of council housing in inner London, 1971–1981' in Clapham, D. and English, J. (Eds), *Public Housing: Current Trends and Future Developments*.

Harloe, M. (1985), *Private Rented Housing in the United States and Europe*, London, Croom Helm.

Hendershot, P. and Hu, S.C. (1981), 'Inflation and extraordinary returns on owner–occupied housing: some implications for capital allocation and productivity growth', *Journal of Macroeconomics*, **3**, 177–203.

Hendry, D.F. (1984), 'Econometric modelling of house prices in the UK', in Hendry, D.F. and Wallis, K.F. (Eds), *Econometrics and Quantitative Economics*, Oxford, Basil Blackwell.

Hendry, D.F. and Ungern–Sternberg, T. (1981), 'Liquidity and inflation effects on consumers' expenditure', chapter 9 in Deaton, A.S. (Ed.),

Essays in the Theory and Measurement of Consumers' Behaviour, Cambridge University Press.

Hills, J. (1988), 'Twenty–first century housing subsidies: durable rent–fixing and subsidy arrangements for social housing', Welfare State Programme Discussion Paper no. 33, London, London School of Economics.

Holmans, A. (1986), 'Flows of funds associated with house purchase for owner–occupation in the United Kingdom 1977–1984 and equity withdrawal from house purchase finance', Government Economic Service Working Paper no. 92.

Holmans, A. (1987), *Housing Policy in Britain: A History*, London, Croom Helm.

Holmans, A. (1988), 'House prices', Department of the Environment, mimeo.

House of Commons Environment Committee (1982), *The Private Rented Sector*, Volumes 1, 2 and 3, HC 40–I,II and III, London, HMSO.

Housing Corporation (1988a), *Circular 31/88*, London, The Corporation.

Housing Corporation (1988b), *Circular 02/88*, London, The Corporation.

Hughes, G. (1988), *Is there Life after the Community Charge?* London, Adam Smith Institute.

Hughes, G.A. and McCormick, B. (1981), 'Do council housing policies reduce migration between regions?' *Economic Journal*, **91**, 919–39.

Hughes, G.A. and McCormick, B. (1985), 'Migration intentions in the UK. Which households want to migrate and which succeed?' *Economic Journal*, **95**, supplement, 113–23.

Hughes, G.A. and McCormick, B. (1987), 'Housing markets, unemployment and labour market flexibility in the UK', *European Economic Review*, **31**, 615–45.

Jenkins, R. (1986), *Racism and Recruitment*, Cambridge University Press.

Johnson, J.H., Salt, J. and Wood, P.A. (1974), *Housing and Migration of Labour in England and Wales*, Farnborough, Saxon House.

Karn, V., Kemeny, J. and Williams, P. (1985), *Home Ownership in the Inner City: Salvation or Despair?* Aldershot, Gower.

Kau, J.B. and Keenan, D. (1983), 'Inflation, taxes and housing: a theoretical analysis', *Journal of Public Economics*, **21**, no.1, June, 93–104.

Kemp, P. (1988a), *The Future of Private Renting*, Salford, Environmental Health and Housing Division, University of Salford.

Kemp, P. (1988b), *The Private Provision of Rented Housing*, Aldershot, Avebury.

King, M. (1988), 'Tax reform: the next step', LSE Financial Markets Group Discussion Paper no. 42, November.

Kleinman, M.P. and Whitehead, C.M.E. (1988), 'The prospects for private renting in the 1990s' in Kemp, P.(Ed.) (1988b).

Law, C. (1980), *Regional Development in the UK since World War I*, Hutchinson.

Layard, P.R.G. and Nickell, S. (1986), 'Unemployment in Britain', *Economica*, **33**, supplement, S121–70.

London Planning Advisory Committee (1988), Unpublished data from *Housing*

Access Study, Commissioned by LPAC.

London Research Centre (1988), *Access to Housing in London*, London, LRC.

McCormick, B. (1989), 'Comment on Bover, Muellbauer and Murphy' in *Oxford Bulletin of Economic and Statistics*, forthcoming.

Markandya, A. and Pemberton, M. (1984), 'The estimation of a disequilibrium model of the housing market – an application to the United Kingdom', University College London Discussion Paper 84–115.

Mayes, D.G. (1979), *The Property Boom: the Effects of Building Society Behaviour on House Prices*, Oxford, Martin Robertson.

Meen, G.P. (1985), 'An econometric analysis of mortgage rationing', Government Economic Service Working Paper no. 79, July.

Meen, G.P. (1987), 'The removal of mortgage market constraints and the implications for econometric modelling of UK house prices', HM Treasury, mimeo.

Meen, G.P. (1988a), 'The ending of mortgage rationing and its effects on the housing market: a simulation study', mimeo, Urban Studies.

Meen, G.P. (1988b), 'The removal of mortgage market constraints and the implications for econometric modelling of UK house prices', mimeo.

Meen, G.P., Mellis, C. and Pain, N. (1987), 'The Treasury slim model project', paper presented to the Macroeconomic Modelling Seminar, University of Warwick, July.

Minford, P., Peel, M. and Ashton, P. (1987), *The Housing Morass*, London, Hobart.

Minford, P., Ashton, P. and Peel, M. (1988), 'The effects of housing distortions on unemployment', *Oxford Economic Papers*, 40, 322–45.

Modigliani, F. and Brumberg, R. (1952), 'Utility analysis and the consumption function: an attempt at integration', reprinted in Abel (Ed.)(1979) *The Collected Papers of Franco Modigliani*, vol.2, MIT Press.

Molho, I.I. (1984), 'A dynamic model of interregional migration flows in Great Britain', *Journal of Regional Science*, 24, 317–37.

Molho, I.I. and Gordon, I.R. (1987), 'The changing pattern of inter–regional migration in Great Britain 1960–86', Regional Science Association, British Section conference, University of Stirling.

Muellbauer, J. (1986), 'Productivity and competitiveness in British manufacturing', *Oxford Review of Economic Policy*, 2, Autumn i–xxv.

Muellbauer, J. (1987), 'The Community Charge, rates and tax reform', *Lloyds Bank Review*, October, 7–19.

Muellbauer, J. and Murphy, A. (1988a), 'Housing and regional migration to and from the south east', mimeo, Nuffield College, Oxford.

Muellbauer, J. and Murphy, A. (1988b), 'House prices and migration: economic and investment implications', Shearson, Lehmann and Hutton Securities research report, December.

Muellbauer, J. and Murphy, A. (1989), 'Why has UK personal saving collapsed?' mimeo.

Nellis, J.G. and Longbottom, J.A. (1981), 'An empirical analysis of the determination of house prices in the United Kingdom', *Urban Studies*, 18, February, 9–21.

Neutze, M. (1987), 'The supply of land for a particular use', *Urban Studies*, **24**, pp.379–88.

Olsen, E.O. (1972), 'An econometric analysis of rent control', *Journal of Political Economy*, **80**, pp.1081–100.

OPCS (1983), *Census* 1981, *Housing and Households, England and Wales*, London, HMSO.

OPCS (1987), *General Household Survey*, 1985, London, HMSO.

Paley, B. (1978), *Attitudes to Letting in* 1976, London, HMSO.

Randolf, W. and Lewis, A. (1988), *Grants, Rents and Subsidies, Research Update*, London, NFHA.

Schaaf, A.H. (1958), 'Federal mortgage interest policy and the supply of FHA–VA credit', *Review of Economic Studies*, November.

Social Housing (1989), 'BES issues: update table', volume 1, no. 3, January.

Spencer, P. (1988), 'The Community Charge and its likely effects on the UK economy', Credit Suisse First Boston, May.

Summers, L.H. (1981), 'Inflation, the stock market and owner–occupied housing', *American Economic Review*, Papers and Proceedings, May, 429–34.

Todd, J., (1988), 'Recent private lettings' in Kemp, P. (Ed.) (1988b), *op. cit.*

Todd, J.E. and Foxon, J. (1987), *Recent Private Lettings* 1982–84, London, HMSO.

Topel, R. and Rosen, S. (1988), 'Housing investment in the United States, *Journal of Political Economy*, **96**, pp.718–40.

Vipond, M.J. (1969), 'Fluctuations in private housebuilding in Great Britain, 1950–1966', *Scottish Journal of Political Economy*, June.

Wadhwani, S. (1986), 'Inflation, bankruptcy, default premia and the stock market', *Economic Journal*, **96**, 120–38.

Weibull, J. (1983), 'A dynamic model of trade frictions and disequilibrium in the housing market', *Scandinavian Journal of Economics*, 372–92.

Whitehead, C.M.E. (1979), 'Why owner–occupation?', *CES Review* no.6.

Whitehead, C.M.E. and Kleinman, M.P. (1986), *Private Rented Housing in the 1980s and 1990s*, Cambridge, Granta Publications.

Whitehead, C.M.E. and Kleinman, M.P. (1987), 'Private renting in London: is it so different?' *Journal of Social Policy*, July.

Whitehead, C.M.E. and Kleinman, M.P. (1988), 'Capital value rents: an evaluation' in Kemp, P. (Ed.) (1988b), *op. cit.*

Wiltshaw, D.G. (1988), 'Pedagogic comment and the supply of land for a particular use', *Urban Studies*, **25**, pp.439–47.

Other publications by NIESR

The National Institute of Economic and Social Research

publishes regularly

The National Institute Economic Review
A quarterly analysis of the general economic situation in the United Kingdom and the world overseas, with forecasts eighteen months ahead. The last issue each year contains an assessment of medium–term prospects. There are also in most issues special articles on subject of interest to academic and business economists.

Annual subscriptions, £55.00 (home), and £75.00 (abroad), also single issues for the current year, £15.00 (home), and £22.00 (abroad), are available directly from NIESR, 2 Dean Trench Street, Smith Square, London, SW1P 3HE.

Subscriptions at the special reduced price of £22.00 p.a. are available to students in the United Kingdom and Irish Republic on application to the Secretary of the Institute.

Back issues and reprints of issues which have gone out of stock are obtainable from Wm Dawson & Sons Ltd, Cannon House, Park Farm Road, Folkestone, Kent. Microfiche copies for the years 1959–88 are available from EP Microform Ltd, Bradford Road, East Ardsley, Wakefield, West Yorkshire, WF3 2AT.

Published by Gower Publishing Company
Education and Economic Performance
Edited by GDN WORSWICK, 1984, pp.152, £21.00 net.

Housing and the National Economy

Energy Self—Sufficiency for the UK
Edited by ROBERT BELGRAVE and MARGARET CORNELL, 1985, pp.224, £19.50 ne

The Future of British Defence Policy
Edited by JOHN ROPER, 1985, pp.214, £24.00 net.

Energy Management: Can We Learn from Others ∩
GEORGE F. RAY, 1985, pp.131, £19.50 net.

Unemployment and Labour Market Policies
Edited by P.E. HART, 1986, pp.230, £24.00 net.

New Priorities in Public Spending
Edited by M.S. LEVITT, 1987, pp.136, £19.50 net.

Policymaking with Macroeconomic Models
Edited by ANDREW BRITTON, 1989, pp.289, £29.50 net.

Published by The Cambridge University Press

Economic and Social Studies

XIX *The Antitrust Laws of the USA: A Study of Competition Enforced by Law*, by A.D. NEALE and D.G. GOYDER. 3rd edn, 1980, pp.548, £50.00 net.

XXI *Industrial Growth and World Trade: An Empirical Study of Trends in Production, Consumption and Trade in Manufactures from 1899—1959 with a Discussion of Probable Future Trends*, by ALFRED MAIZELS. Reprinted with corrections, 1971, pp.563, £22.50 net.

XXV *Exports and Economic Growth of Developing Countries*, by ALFRED MAIZELS, assisted by L.F. CAMPBELL–BOROSS and P.B.W. RAYMENT, 1968, pp.445, £20.00 net.

XXVII *The Framework of Regional Economics in the United Kingdom*, by A.J. BROWN, 1972, pp.372, £22.50 net.

XXVIII *The Structure, Size and Costs of Urban Settlements*, by P.A. STONE, 1973, pp.304, £18.50 net.

XXIX *The Diffusion of New Industrial Processes: An International Study*, edited by L. NABSETH and G.F. RAY, 1974, pp.346, £22.50 net.

XXXI *British Economic Policy*, 1960—74, edited by F.T. BLACKABY, 1978, pp.710, £40.00 net.

XXXII *Industrialisation and the Basis for Trade*, by R.A. BATCHELOR, R.L. MAJOR and A.D. MORGAN, 1980, pp.380, £30.00 net.

XXXIV *World Inflation since 1950. An International Comparative Study*, by A.J. BROWN assisted by JANE DARBY, 1985, pp.428, £35.00 net.

Other publications by NIESR

Occasional Papers

XXXI *Diversification and Competition*, by M.A. UTTON, 1979, pp.124, £13.50 net.

XXXII *Concentration in British Industry*, 1935–75, by P.E. HART and R. CLARKE, 1980, pp.178, £19.50 net.

XXXIV *International Industrial Productivity*, by A.D. SMITH, D.M.W.N. HITCHENS and S.W. DAVIES, 1982, pp.184, £25.00 net.

XXXV *Concentration and Foreign Trade*, by M.A. UTTON and A.D. MORGAN, 1983, pp.150, £22.50 net.

XXXVI *The Diffusion of Mature Technologies*, by GEORGE F. RAY, 1984, pp.96, £19.50 net.

XXXVII *Productivity in the Distributive Trades. A Comparison of Britain, America and Germany*, by A.D. SMITH and D.M.W.N. HITCHENS, 1985, pp.160, £25.00 net.

XXXVIII *Profits and Stability of Monopoly*, by M.A. UTTON, 1986, pp.102, £15.00 net.

XXXIX *The Trade Cycle in Britain*, 1958–1982, by ANDREW BRITTON, 1986, pp.108, £15.00 net.

XL *Britain's Productivity Gap*, by STEPHEN DAVIES and RICHARD E. CAVES, 1987, pp.149, £19.50 net.

XLI *The Growth and Efficiency of Public Spending*, by M.S. LEVITT and M.A.S. JOYCE, 1987, pp.211, £25.00 net.

XLII *British Imports of Consumer Goods. A Study of Import Penetration* 1974–85, by ANN D. MORGAN, 1988, pp.140, £19.50 net.

XLIII *Youth Unemployment in Great Britain*, by P.E. HART, 1988, pp.155, £19.50 net.

NIESR Students' Edition

2. *The Antitrust Laws of the U.S.A.* (3rd edition, unabridged), by A.D. NEALE and D.G. GOYDER, 1980, pp.548, £19.50 net.

4. *British Economic Policy*, 1960–74: *Demand Management* (an abridged version of *British Economic Policy*, 1960–74), edited by F.T. BLACKABY, 1979, pp.472, £17.50 net.

5. *The Evolution of Giant Firms in Britain* (2nd impression with a new preface), by S.J. PRAIS, 1981, pp.344, £11.95 net.